SUSTAINABILITY IS THE FUTURE

SUSTAINABILITY IS THE FUTURE

Tay Kay Luan

PARTRIDGE

Copyright © 2020 by Tay Kay Luan.

ISBN: Softcover   978-1-5437-5899-3
            eBook   978-1-5437-5900-6

All rights reserved. No part of this book may be used or reproduced by any means, graphic, electronic, or mechanical, including photocopying, recording, taping or by any information storage retrieval system without the written permission of the author except in the case of brief quotations embodied in critical articles and reviews.

Because of the dynamic nature of the Internet, any web addresses or links contained in this book may have changed since publication and may no longer be valid. The views expressed in this work are solely those of the author and do not necessarily reflect the views of the publisher, and the publisher hereby disclaims any responsibility for them.

Print information available on the last page.

To order additional copies of this book, contact
Toll Free 800 101 2657 (Singapore)
Toll Free 1 800 81 7340 (Malaysia)
orders.singapore@partridgepublishing.com

www.partridgepublishing.com/singapore

For Linden

CONTENTS

Foreword ix
Preface..xiii
Acknowledgements xxiii
Introduction xxv

1. The Future 1
2. Denials... 13
3. Politics 25
4. Justice 36
5. Challenges 42
6. Opportunities..50
7. Compliance 61
8. Health 68
9. Food Security 75
10. Responsible Investment 80
11. Electric Vehicles 88
12. Going Robotic 95
13. The Plastic Menace 102
14. Maldives Challenges 113
15. New Normal Behaviours 123
16. Youth 132
17. Education 140

18.	Risks	149
19.	Attitudes	156
20.	Convergence	163

About the Authors 175

FOREWORD

I write this foreword against the difficult backdrop of the Covid-19 pandemic and the sombre realisation that our global systems must change. Seldom before have we seen a single event exert such an influence upon the interdependency of our environment, health, well-being, and socio-economic systems. The urgent need for reform and collective engagement could not be clearer for us all to see.

We were not prepared for this pandemic. Our blatant disregard for global stewardship and our unreadiness to take collective responsibility for our actions to secure a sustainable context for future generations is alarming. Time is not on our side. We need to critically reflect and act.

This is the third volume Tay Kay Luan has published on the theme of sustainability. His clear and analytical overview reaffirms the need to engage in a far more holistic approach as we set realistic goals to address the challenges of climate change and the requirements placed upon us as we start our journey through a post-Covid recovery stage. A key feature throughout his analysis is the importance of championing a 'green recovery' strategy, thus placing sustainable goals at the core of our economic and social development plans. The global challenges facing agriculture, climate change, and biodiversity, to name only a few, demonstrate the need for individuals to take ownership of green change-management strategies. The collective responsibility placed upon us all as we rebuild our communities is to deconstruct our traditional value systems and make a clear commitment to delivering upon the sustainable goals which are so clearly demonstrated in this volume.

Throughout this volume, Tay Kay Luan reaffirms the importance of articulating a discourse which places green disruptive intervention at the heart of our socio-economic and political engagement. We need to activate a generation of disruptive leaders who can connect with societal and environmental change for humankind to reform our ecosystem in a way which allows for opportunity and survival. What I am referring to here is the importance of a socio-environmental capital which can be used to further a common good and reaffirm our fundamental humanity. This volume revisits the deeply rooted relationship between humans and their natural world and the value of a collective stewardship which binds them together on a common course of action.

What we will be facing together in the post-Covid recovery period will be a far greater awareness of the value of universal compassion. We must start with ourselves and question what makes a balanced life where mutual respect and deep appreciation of the universal is at the core of our thinking. A greater appreciation of causality will be required and an honest engagement with the way we must work upon ourselves, our behaviour, and our thinking to respond to the natural world.

It is always difficult to get people to change, be it patterns of behaviour or cultural norms linked to group values. Wars are the direct result of change failure. The challenge ahead will be to articulate a common direction of travel, a universal direction which gives a sense of belonging and purpose. That purpose must be articulated within a language framework that sees the importance of mutual respect, causality of action towards the natural world, and compassion towards the other within our society. The quest is to liberate ourselves so that we can see anew the wonder, value, and purpose of a common humanity and well-being.

It is of particular importance to me as the vice chancellor of the University of Wales that my own government was the first to legislate a Well-Being of Future Generations Act, which gives a clear legal obligation to improve upon social, cultural, environmental, and economic well-being. It requires all public bodies within the country to think anew about the long-term impact of decisions and to work better with people, communities, and each other in order to address a range of persistent problems such as poverty, health inequalities, and climate change.

The same core values articulated in the Wales Act are the ones discussed by Tay Kay Luan in *Sustainability Is the Future*. The focus is upon resilience and developing a far greater appreciation of what can be achieved to support the common good and a sustainable future. In his introduction, the author states that 'sustainable development goals have given global communities and individuals a vision of the future, clarity of purpose, a responsibility for stakeholders to embrace, and a commitment for all to participate.' His volume offers an excellent oversight of how human well-being depends upon maintaining a balanced ecosystem where mutual respect for nature is seen.

We must learn how to view the world through a lens of ecology, where the people and planet matter equally. This will mean exploring alternative economic models built upon common goals and values which place stewardship and a commitment to safeguarding our future at the core of our decision-making. We are part of a natural order, and it is incumbent upon us all to respect and promote those sustainable values which offer us all a better world.

> Professor Medwin Hughes, DL, FRSA, FLSW
> Vice Chancellor, the University of Wales
> The University of Wales: Trinity Saint David

PREFACE

The establishment of the World Commission on Environment and Development (WCED) in 1983 led to the publication in 1987 of *Our Common Future*, also known as the Brundtland Report. This brought global attention to the concept of sustainable development, which was defined as development that meets the needs of the present without compromising the ability of future generations to meet their own needs. *Sustainability* is a term that means different things to different people. To some, it is an excuse to do nothing, while for others, it is a rallying cry.

Like apple pie and cream, who could object to such a wide-reaching notion as sustainability? It is because of its fluffy nature that there has been slow progress in changing the economic driver and the way we do business. However, as with everything, it is not about agreement. It is all about implementation. The author has brought a refreshing perspective to sustainability in that he has been a successful businessman and is now an academic and author. It is his business background that enables him to rethink and reconceptualise the problem and ask questions that matter. In my opinion, because the author, Tay Kay Luan, is not afraid to question the way things are done and suggest alternatives, this book shows there can be a real possibility of progress in 2020, thirty-three years after the Brundtland Report was first published. This is because of the increased profile of climate change, despite the global impact of Covid-19.

The book starts with the author questioning what the future holds for sustainability. It is important to recognise that sustainability has both spatial and temporal dimensions. These impact on socio-economic policies, with an example being coastal development. It is seen as a good investment opportunity, but with climate change comes storms and sea-level rise. Therefore, investments are at risk, and future generations will have to make the hard decision of whether or not to defend them. These tensions are recognised as the author draws the reader into his thought processes. He weaves the academic storyline in a way that will connect with a wide variety of readers, including experts and the uninformed.

Chapter 2 focuses on denials, and this is important, because since the millennium there has been a change in both investors' and the general population's perceptions of environmental harm. For example, ExxonMobil is facing a lawsuit over ignoring risks related to climate change, while many other companies are subjected to meetings where shareholders push the industry towards more progressive positions on climate change. Shareholders are pressuring oil companies to act and calling for greater transparency on corporate social responsibility, including emissions and alignment with the Paris Agreement.

Chapter 3 seamlessly continues the author's argument as he considers the politics of climate change. With socio-economic priorities, policies come to the forefront and politicians take positions. However, when policies are no more than optional guidelines, there is no mandate to comply, and therefore, despite a paradigm shift, companies do not necessarily follow. For example, JPMorgan recently rejected shareholder calls to disclose its full carbon footprint. So even under an increased focus on climate change, with some responding to resolutions, there is still resistance to change.

Therefore, there is a call for justice (chapter 4), which positions global warming as both an ethical and political issue rather than just environmental or physical. Importantly, climate justice relates climate change effects to concepts of environmental justice and social justice, and deals with issues such as equality, human rights, collective rights, and historical responsibilities for climate change. It is the latter that the author recognises as being a barrier for change, and once again, his narrative relates the need for doing things differently.

Everyone who is old enough to understand will always remember Covid-19, a pandemic which for the first time in living memory brought the economy to a stop. As the author relates, restrictions were introduced globally on people's movement, national borders were closed, schools were shut, and all nonessential services were halted. His references to the pandemic and climate change as both being issues needing global response is well made and justified.

Challenges (chapter 5) and the pandemic experience (chapter 6) show the author's business guile in recognising opportunities whilst he academically highlights greenhouse gas reductions in the lockdown. Pandemic consequences have turned the lights out in many large cities, whilst working from home became the new norm. Lessons of past pandemics led to changes in city planning, and once again town planners are looking to overcome problems such as by increasing space for cyclists, a social-distanced form of transport.

The reader is brought back to business mode in chapter 7 on compliance. As businesses face more restrictions on the materials they use, PricewaterhouseCoopers (PwC) identified governance incorporating sustainability as the way to manage risk and ensure compliance. National and international companies operating in different territories find navigating governance, risk, and compliance problematic. By assessing opportunities and risks, the author identifies education; housing; job creation; and setting the right institutional framework, governance, and management as necessary for effective implementation of sustainable development goals. Legal requirements, company policies, and industry-specific and voluntary codes are needed to improve future compliance.

The book then addresses significant future challenges with health concerns (chapter 8) and food security (chapter 9). In developed countries, there is a recognised increase in chronic diseases, obesity, and mental health problems, as well as worsening environmental problems. It has been argued that inadequate integration of health promotion and sustainability at local, regional, and global levels has caused many of these health and sustainability problems. Predictions of future healthcare costs have forced governments to develop initiatives at both national and international levels to promote healthy and sustainable living.

There have also been environmental problems caused by food production: for example, intensive agriculture and farming practices. Therefore, food security and food inequalities have focused the political agenda on the health and sustainability of a food system which is market-driven. Subsequently, the author links many different factors contributing to health and food security, as well as consequences such as conflict, natural disasters, and widening income gaps. All will cause mass movements of people and result in future refugee crises and further challenges for food security and health. However, as with all aspects of this book, the author gives hope for the future, including eloquently justifying carbon reduction.

The author returns to a focused business perspective in chapter 10 on responsible investment. Adoption of environmental, social, and governance dimensions in private investments has evolved from risk management, where future innovation and new opportunities create long-term value for business and society. This encourages more private investment in sustainable development, where sustainable investing focuses on enterprises that seek to address social, environmental, and governance concerns. Investment value chains—including investors, banks, and companies—commonly include environmental, social, and governance (ESG) criteria when screening potential investments, using sustainability information in their reporting processes. A number of principle-based, voluntary ESG initiatives are gaining traction throughout the private investment chain. These include UNEP finance initiatives with over 200 institutions including banks, insurers, and fund managers; sustainability insurance, providing a framework for innovative risk management and insurance solutions; and a Sustainable Stock Exchanges Initiative. Working with investors, regulators, and companies to enhance corporate transparency and ESG performance, the latter encourages responsible long-term investments through a peer-to-peer learning platform.

The sustainability journey continues with chapter 11 on electric vehicles, where the author focuses his narrative on the contribution of technological change. The business case needs support, because for many battery manufacturers, operating margins are negative with volatile cash flows. Therefore, electric vehicles are not having the major growth they deserve due to inadequate advancement in battery technology. Currently, battery packs cannot be charged as quickly as previously anticipated, and there is a lack of charging stations. Added to this, battery prices are expected to increase by about 20 per cent over the coming years, despite prices of raw materials such as cobalt and lithium plummeting due to lower demand. A recent Goldman Sachs report highlighted that clear progress in battery technology could bring down the cost of electric vehicles by 30 to 40 per cent, although to make a breakthrough, consumers will need adequate subsidies and incentives.

In chapter 12, 'Going Robotic', the author once again crafts a persuasive narrative, this time linking robotic contributions to the future of sustainability. The chapter once again connects previous and current topics as the narrative develops between robotic solutions, electric cars, the transformation of business, and the mobility and connectivity of people. We are all familiar with increasing automation of industrial processes and the use of robotics, sensors, and twenty-four-hour continuous production. Robotics improve productivity, reduce energy use, and cut waste generation in the commercial process, thereby delivering clear sustainability benefits. Artificial intelligence and real-time applications mean that in the future, going robotic will not require so much human interface.

As part of a roller-coaster ride, the author once again brings the reader face to face with an environmental problem. This time, in chapter 13, 'The Plastic Menace', he considers a material that became indispensable due to its versatility but has become a problem due to its ubiquitous presence in the environment. There are limitations to completely getting rid of plastic waste, despite alternative materials and capacities to recycle. All lands and oceans are polluted to some extent by plastics, and in June 2020, newspaper headlines declared that plastic rain is the new acid rain. CNN reported that 11 billion tonnes of plastic is expected to accumulate in the environment by 2025, much of it ending up as a pollutant. Scientists found that more than 1,000 tonnes of microplastic particles falls onto national parks and protected lands in the western US annually, and scientists discovered that these secondary plastics are present in nearly every ecosystem on the planet. Banning single-use plastics should be only the start, because the impact of plastic on biodiversity is far from clear.

The author continues his environmental considerations in chapter 14 on the Maldives, where he highlights the difficulties of being sustainable when there are significant economic, social, and environmental challenges. A small island developing state, the Maldives is geographically isolated, with a dispersed population, and this results in limited potential for economies of scale. Therefore, high transaction costs and climate change vulnerabilities impose economic limitations on a widespread population. Waste management is one of the biggest challenges in the Maldives, so consequently, the focus is to avoid creating any waste in the first place. For example, suppliers are encouraged to reduce packaging when delivering supplies and ordering in bulk whenever possible; ban single-use plastics; and recycle all organic waste. Implementation of sustainable development goals (SDGs) in the Maldives will be built upon its successes implementing the Millennium Development Goals.

In chapter 15 on 'New Normal Behaviours', the author brings business and consumer perspectives to a transformed landscape. He articulates the debate on challenges and commitment in the context of prevailing concerns on choices and priorities. The new normal will demand adoption of things learned through Covid-19. With renewed vigour, the author advocates for the simple use of video-conferencing facilities and replacing throwaway culture with a reusable and recyclable lifestyle. This latter point leads nicely into the next dilemma concerning the youth (chapter 16). The author recognises a contradiction, in that amongst the young there is generally an awareness of the environment and sustainability issues, yet some fully engage in the throwaway culture. Despite this, there is always hope, because as the author recognises, there is a willingness to change.

Chapter 17 on education looks at the means by which sustainability change can be brought about. It is no accident that this follows the chapter on influencing the youth. Education for Sustainable Development (ESD) empowers people to work towards a sustainable future with an integrated approach. The book recognises its role in transforming society by helping people develop knowledge, skills, values, and behaviours needed for sustainable development. UNESCO wants to improve access to quality education on sustainable development for all societies and at all levels. It is about including issues such as climate change and biodiversity in teaching and learning and educating people to respect cultural diversity, which will contribute to a more sustainable world. As recognised by the author, the right institutional framework, governance, and management strategies are required for effective implementation of sustainable development.

In chapter 18 on risks, the author's play on words alerts the reader to the risk and challenges of doing nothing. Many potential causes of human conflict that will lead to loss of life and new refugee crises include food security, fresh water and energy, and sustainability challenges requiring broader assessments of social and climate risks. Interestingly, he links climate concern and risk, arguing that resolution will require the same energy, commitment, and resources that were needed to overcome Covid-19. However, for the reader, a clear argument is made for the risk of severe consequences should nothing be done.

In chapter 19, the author demonstrates the need to change attitudes. He again seamlessly weaves a link between business and sustainability. Many global surveys on attitudes have been undertaken, and a recent Asian report analysed and presented data for fourteen Asian markets. Insights yielded subjective perceptions, attitudes, preferences, and buying behaviours of Asian consumers related to sustainability. Because of the importance of Asia as a manufacturing export hub, changing sustainability attitudes of consumers in Europe, the United States, and elsewhere will significantly impact Asian local business and operating practices.

Chapter 20, 'Convergence', is the final chapter, and as the title suggests, this is where the author brings things together. For a successful transition towards sustainability, it is necessary to understand sustainability-related knowledge, attitude, and practice (KAP). A systematic review of the ten KAP sustainability studies in the scientific literature between 1990 and 2016 found that half were conducted in educational environments. KAP results varied among the studies, and there was a general tendency to investigate aspects related to ecosystems, natural resources, environmental protection, and conservation. Studies of global climate change and sea-level rise have been used to determine flooding and erosion risk, while adaptation strategies and measures have been proposed for flood prevention and mitigation.

In conclusion, *Sustainability Is the Future* is a credit to author Tay Kay Luan. His persuasive arguments will make readers believe in his way forward, because as he says, to do nothing is a cold reminder of the future risk and challenges we could face.

Professor Michael R. Phillips
Former Pro Vice Chancellor, the University of Wales
The University of Wales: Trinity Saint David

ACKNOWLEDGEMENTS

I am very thankful to Professor Medwin Hughes for writing the foreword, Professor Michael R. Phillips for introducing the topics in the preface, and Zubair Hassan for his contribution to the chapter on the Maldives.

INTRODUCTION

The lockdown of major cities and restrictions on people's movement to halt the spread of Covid-19 caused significant social and economic disruptions during the first half of the year 2020. The global impact has forced many governments to resort to economic stimulus for individuals and businesses to rough out the tough time ahead. Despite that, many businesses have been forced to close, resulting in thousands being laid off. The scale of disruption was unimaginable, especially since in some cases, the global pandemic stretched the public capacity to cope and respond and exposed inherent weaknesses in both resources and infrastructures.

The global pandemic demonstrated the damage it could do to the fragile economic and social fabric of nations. There is no denying that repercussions of rising unemployment and social discontent are sustainability concerns. Climate-related impacts and new infections will not make matters any better. Issues related to climate change, increasing destruction of biodiversity and forestry, and the widening gap between rich and poor, among others, will continue to top the agenda and priorities of political and community leaders.

Warnings

The report, *The Future Is Now: Science for Achieving Sustainable Development*, prepared by an independent group of scientists, has made global leaders and members aware of the tipping points ahead. These negatives, in the opinion of the scientists, will lead to dramatic changes to the environmental conditions of the planet.

Such warnings are in line with what was said in *The World Bank Report on Climate Change Action Plan 2016–20*, which recognised the enormous challenge of climate change to fragile economies and societies. The global institution reported that by the year 2050, the planet will have to feed 9 billion people, extend housing and services to 2 billion new urban residents, and provide universal access to affordable energy while bringing down global greenhouse gas emissions to a level that makes a sustainable future possible.

Not many will disagree with the fact the sustainability challenges of the future lie not only in the understanding of the concept and changes but the irreversible consequences. Take, for example, the case of climate change, where scientists and experts have repeatedly said that global greenhouse gas emissions have exceeded the limits, with consequences including melting ice, rising sea levels, floods, volatile weather, and forest fires. Threats to food security, access to fresh water, and affordable energy carry severe risks for human conflicts, bringing unnecessary loss of life and renewed waves of refugees.

The global pandemic that has kept many national leaders awake and concerned over an uncertain future has been a major distraction from the wider economic, political, and social challenges of sustainability. Climate change and the Covid-19 pandemic share a number of commonalities that threaten humanity. Pandemics and climate concerns both have socio-economic impacts that can seem unimaginable. McKinsey & Company sees a similarity in that both could unleash exogenous and external shocks to economies as well as disruption to the supply chain and global distribution mechanisms.

Indeed, experts have forecast that by the year 2050, there is no guarantee that all people will have a roof over their heads, access to clean water, and proper health and sanitary needs. If the world does nothing, there are already predictions of frequent floods, droughts, sea-level rise, water shortages, threats to food security, and the frequency of natural disasters, especially forest fires. Such threats inevitably put millions at risk of becoming climate refugees or victims of renewed conflicts.

Policies

There is now an urgent need for greener policies, as advances in science and technological research have enabled better adaptation for local use and application. There is much to do. Transitioning to cleaner energy requires more effort, especially in a diverse environment.

Not all the 180 countries which made pledges on climate action have rectified their treaties. The withdrawal of the United States from the Paris Agreement towards lowering carbon emissions was a low point, but not a single country which made the pledges in 2016 has fulfilled its promise. More ambitious targets for 2030 are to be discussed and agreed upon at the next climate conference scheduled for Glasgow in 2021.

Not everything is gloom and doom. Debate on sustainability resources and responsibilities will continue once the coronavirus pandemic is under control. Right up to

January 2020, all eyes were on the United Nations' organised climate conference. The global pandemic has offered a fresh window of opportunity for nations to shape the future of sustainability.

Lessons to Learn

If there is one lesson world leaders can learn from this pandemic crisis, it is the return of nature and ecology. Obvious effects can be observed from the lockdown of economic activities. Immediate improvements in air quality have been observed in major cities from New York to New Delhi. In China, scientists have observed a drop in nitrogen dioxide in the air of as much as 30 per cent. With cars missing from the highways and factories shut, carbon emissions have naturally come down.

The most significant change has been the reduction in carbon emissions from a drastic drop in air travel. It was also obvious that with empty highways, there was hardly any air pollution reported in all the major cities. In the waterways at Venice, dolphins were sighted, signalling a drop in pollution and human threats.

Change

Understanding the challenges of sustainability will demand acceptance of broader relationships between social, health, and ecological risks and ought to be given the utmost priority as part of the broader government role to do the right thing. Addressing climate concerns, for example, requires the energy, commitment, and resources that were observed during the battle to overcome the spread of the global pandemic. The new normal will demand that governments seriously put sustainable development goals at the heart of policy development.

This is easier said than done. Political leaders will need to be able to see eye to eye and display the moral leadership expected of them. There is a greater need for a coordinated policy action among the global leaders from the 174 countries and European Union represented at the 2016 Paris climate agreement. It is harder without the fiscal means and incentives, especially when oil prices are at an all-time low. There is no better time to remove subsidies for fossil fuel and condition for actions to be taken now. One of the recommendations from *The Future Is Now: Science for Achieving Sustainable Development* is to accelerate the diffusion of renewable energy. Infrastructures need to be overhauled and replaced by renewable energy technology.

This book, *Sustainability Is the Future*, reinforces and supports the view that the future is already here. It recognises the challenges of ensuring a system resilient enough to cope with crises on a global scale, be they climate- or health-related. These challenges include constant denials of real danger ahead, ensuring preparedness to cope with sudden shocks or educating to change habits and attitudes. All these demand difficult choices within the political, economic, and social context. There are already numerous opinions and comments being expressed and written from the perspectives of policymakers, experts, community leaders, and so on. There is an acceptance of the risks of severe consequences should nothing be done.

The pandemic experience already says it all. There is an ongoing conflict between vested economic and political interests, conveniences, and legacies. Even at the international level, there is a global stand and need to engage in a common war, be it against a pandemic or climate change. The reactions from governmental leaders were swift in some cases. As the global pandemic spread, within weeks schools and factories were shut, and most workers were asked to stay home.

Sustainability Is the Future would be a reminder to readers that key sustainability themes have not gone away amid the pandemic confusion. The book explores the challenges surrounding the goal of 'holding the increase in the global average temperature to well below 2 °C above preindustrial level' agreed to by every United Nations member nation in the 2016 Paris climate agreement. The United States, however, has since pulled out from the agreement.

The debate on challenges is not one of commitment alone. There are prevailing concerns over choices and priorities at both the national and grassroots level. Discussion is not just on what we can learn from the pandemic crisis, the opportunities that come with it, and the lessons that can be avoided. There are real fears that windows of opportunity could be shut as fast as they were opened.

Indeed, threats of worsening food security, widening income gaps, and increased conflicts of priorities continue to pose sustainability challenges. These health, social, and economic challenges demand greater partnership on a global scale. There is optimism about the future, and therefore, it is likely we could possibly experience forces of change that include converging technologies, making it easier for conveniences to be sustained, dangers to be removed, and demands of markets and societies to be delivered upon. While there are limitations—for example, elimination of plastic waste—there are improved substitutions and increased capacity to recycle. Renewable technologies are more accessible and affordable, learning has been made easier through digital means, and robotic solutions and electric cars are set to transform business and the mobility and connectivity of people.

Vision

Sustainability Is the Future presses home the point that sustainable development goals have given global communities and individuals a vision of the future, clarity of purpose, a responsibility for stakeholders to embrace, and a commitment for all to participate. It is within this context that the role of government is being re-emphasised. In recognising that governments alone cannot be the only stakeholder to push for change, the importance and contributions of others must be acknowledged.

Shaping the directions will demand collective and coherent actions from every single stakeholder. Scientists, researchers, policymakers, businesses, and consumers must not only in embrace policies but also follow through with commitment and consistency. An example is demonstrated in the case of the Maldives, which shows the importance of government to overcome the complexities of sustainability and the challenges ahead.

By the very nature and influence of governments, policymakers and regulators have an important responsibility to push for more in the hope of flattening the climate curve, echoing the opinion of the *Economist* in its issue of 23 May 23 2020. The access and the power vested in leaders to influence and shape political and economic mandates remains the key. At every level, from national to local, governments do have the access to resources and the capacity to steer the execution of these sustainable development goals.

This book intends to give readers a view of the great things to come as well as a cold reminder of the risk and challenges if nothing is done.

CHAPTER 1

The Future

In December 2019, Wall Street investors were filled with optimism for the new year. With stable oil prices at around USD 60 per barrel, many pundits were upbeat over the new year's prospects. Covid-19, which was reported to have started in Wuhan, China, soon became a global pandemic, and its impact on global markets was almost immediate. Within weeks, major stock markets turned bearish, sparking fear in investors that global economies would soon retreat into recession.

Pandemic Impacts and Sustainability

As the number of Covid-19 cases exceeded 30 million worldwide in September 2020 and the number of deaths recorded worldwide passed the 900,000 mark according to the World Health Organisation (WHO), planners and economists expected tougher times ahead. The majority agreed that, because of the shutdown of business in communities worldwide, most major economies would lose at least 2 to 3 per cent of their gross domestic growth, and millions would be laid off.

Governments in all affected countries feared the pandemic would disrupt the supply chain across global economies. The disruption to the supply chain could possibly lead to price distortion. Any nationwide shortage would also lead to escalating prices, a cause of concern not only to the poor but also to the business community. If basic food essentials such as garlic, onions, and rice were held up at their source, it would immediately put pressure on price mechanisms and create unnecessary price increases.

The global oil market's oversupply and dip in oil prices added further economic uncertainty to oil-exporting nations. Falling oil prices would not necessarily put pressure on cost inflation in countries that were dependent on oil revenue. Many business analysts were predicting a tougher economic environment ahead for oil and gas sectors as well as industries such as tourism, hospitality, and retail.

Questions were raised as to whether the sudden shutdown of economic activities would have positive implications for climate concerns. The lockdowns in major cities on most continents in response to the pandemic led to an immediate drop in global carbon emissions, which, according to the International Energy Agency (IEA), fell by a record 8 per cent. The noticeable drop in greenhouse gas emissions and pollution was a direct consequence of the lockdowns, movement restrictions, factory closures, and drastic changes in the transportation sector—including as much as a 10 per cent reduction in the aviation sector.

On 22 April 2020, the *Guardian* reported that this decline in carbon emissions offered a glimpse of an alternative future. The newspaper reported on clear skies, returning wildlife, and other environmental positives as the earth celebrated the fiftieth anniversary of Earth Day.

Climate Change Challenges

A reduction in carbon footprint was evident during the lockdown of cities' transportation systems and human activities. The best way to continue reducing our carbon footprint, though, is to accelerate the drop in the burning of fossil fuels. While the EU has an ambitious target of shifting to alternative renewable energy, there is always a temptation to delay this transition due to the low price of oil and gas. Industrial activities that rely on fossil fuel have caused excessive emission of carbon for decades, leading to global warming. The use of fossil fuel is the main cause of climate change.

Major cities have reported record-breaking temperatures each summer. This trend is worrying, and experts have already witnessed the effects of climate change on the polar regions. Melting ice in both Antarctica and the Arctic is causing sea levels to rise, threatening coastal towns and cities.

If nothing is done to overcome the negative impacts of climate change, the entire earth is sitting on a time bomb. Experts have repeatedly said that warmer weather will have a massive impact on socio-economic aspects of life and will disturb the fragile fabric of many societies. The Intergovernmental Panel on Climate Change (IPCC) has repeatedly warned global leaders that the global temperature is already more than 1.0 °C above preindustrial levels, and the UN body has strongly urged global cooperation to limit increase to no more than 1.5 °C. Despite the agreements at the United Nations–led climate summits to reduce greenhouse gases in the atmosphere, there are challenges or even doubts as to whether leading nations have the will and commitment to fulfil their promises to reduce carbon emissions before the turn of the century.

Naomi Klein, author of *This Changes Everything*, argues that any appropriate response to climate change demands more than political will. She has said on many occasions that the current system will not fix the climate risk. Instead, an overhaul of the market system will be necessary; this includes greater regulation of corporations and greater community activism.

According to the IEA, China, the United States, India, Russia, and Japan are responsible for over half of all fossil fuel-related carbon dioxide emissions. If nothing is done, greenhouse gas will continue to rise, and the earth is expected to warm by another 6.4 °C. It is quite unthinkable that the global leaders and community would accept such a scenario. Global warming has been on the radar of many governments for some time now, and most accept that there are present and future dangers from climate risks. A global pledge to stabilise the climate at no more than a 1.5 °C increase by year 2030 must be delivered upon.

Applying Science and Technology

The widespread application of science and technology is of absolute importance in the war against climate change. Appropriate financing and investment are vital components of this fight. Cleaner technology must be affordable and accessible to the global community, or else it stands no chance of winning the support of the general public.

There are already great examples in technology of renewable energy alternatives in power plants and the transportation sector. The BBC headline 'Britain Goes Coal

Free as Renewables Edge out Fossil Fuels' on 10 June 2020 would have been unthinkable two decades ago. The drastic drop in the demand for coal-fired electricity was partly due to the lockdown of human activities, but more so it is a result of the transformation of the energy system. Today, the country has the world's largest offshore wind energy farm, and this, plus other renewables, makes up almost 40 per cent of the United Kingdom's electricity supply.

Another example of renewable energy is solar energy, which has enjoyed exponential growth in recent years. Solar energy extraction and storage has improved, and the price of solar panels has become more affordable and competitive. China, India, and the United States have all successfully built solar farms to produce solar electricity to meet local demands.

Consumers and businesses demand efficiency, cost effectiveness, convenience, and reliability. It is in this field of renewable energy that governments will need to lead, not only to ensure the widespread availability of financing but to ensure that proper large-scale policies are enacted to make these technologies economical and accessible. Governments must commit to decarbonising energy systems across all sectors: transport, commercial, industrial, and even residential.

Due to its high carbon footprint and pollution, China is committed to being at the forefront of renewable energy. Its power plants still rely on coal, but its leaders are determined to shift to alternative energy. The European Union has already made a commitment to phase out fossil fuel. Its key targets include a 40 per cent cut in greenhouse gas emissions, a 32 per cent share of renewable energy, and a 32 per cent improvement in energy efficiency by the year 2030.

Social Systems

The pandemic has exposed a gap in global conditions and systems, especially the vulnerability of fragile societies which barely have a health system to cope with the large number of people infected with coronavirus. The pandemic has reminded the world of the widening gap between rich and poor, and social deprivations and rising poverty are immediate consequences of the pandemic. The hardest hit in the Covid-19 pandemic are the poor and the front-line workers, who are at the highest risk of contracting the infectious disease.

For the young and healthy, the immediate impact of the pandemic has been the closure of businesses and the immediate loss of jobs. According to the International Labour Organization, as many as 3.3 billion people could potentially see their workplaces fully or partly closed. Restrictions on daily movement have also worsened the conditions. The majority of those who have lost their jobs are semiskilled or unskilled workers. The pandemic revealed the extent of inequality among the socio-economic groups. While many governments have tried to allay fears, many others have committed to digging deeper into their reserves to overcome this challenging economic environment.

UN Sustainable Development Goals

The UN's seventeen sustainable development goals (SDGs) paint a picture of a sustainable future. All member states of the UN are committed to achieving the SDGs, which require them to align their policies and developments to a commitment towards reducing their carbon footprint.

The pandemic may have severely distracted attention away from climate change, but evidence of the broader pandemic's impact on sustainability is obvious. As an example, some 25 million people in the United States could possibly be laid off, with thousands more in the informal sector at risk. There are other concerns coming from threats of a weakened food security system, including a worsening of relative poverty in some constituencies where the health system is weak and vulnerable. The future of sustainability hangs in the balance as governments, businesses, civil societies, international agencies, and nongovernmental organisations cooperate on several initiatives to combat the pandemic and to mitigate its severe consequences.

Concerned over the eventual economic impacts of the virus, governments around the world have announced a series of fiscal assistance, economic stimulus, and support packages to help individuals, businesses, and economies roll over the tough time ahead. Governments' immediate response has been to ensure there was adequate funding available in the system to support people most impacted and to mitigate loss of income and jobs. In many cases, the public sector worked with financial institutions to suspend loan repayment and to allow certain concessions to help ease financial burdens.

Not many will disagree over immediate economic aid. Governments need no reminders that their measures should include fresh opportunities to adopt zero carbon technology in their infrastructure investment. There is no reason why governments should not consider the fresh opportunity to recreate job opportunities in a new low-carbon environment. Ensuring supply chain activities, especially in food distribution, is also important, as this would easily be disrupted by the closure of national borders and transportation systems.

Governments are in the best position to consider or even accelerate appropriate investment towards digital technologies to meet the challenge of how people connect and engage. Indeed, allowing wider access to the internet, for example, allows greater inclusion, and this is available at a low cost.

The increasing use of artificial-intelligence-enabled robotics is feared by many because of the threat to jobs, but there are positive gains to be made from such innovation. It is necessary to put into context the sustainability agenda, where such innovations can be put to good use across industry, people, and society. As an example, enhanced robotics have not only improved efficiency in resource utilisation but have proven their social worth in the deployment of renewable energy and data research in the battle against climate change.

Having a public policy makes a difference not only in embracing a new mindset but also in accepting new habits towards reducing waste. One example is the ban on single-use plastic. No politician will ever say no to good social benefits. The movement to address sustainability should highlight how changes in public policy towards waste or the use of new technology will benefit society.

There are opportunities to accelerate technological progress provided for by the resetting of the economy in many of the advanced markets badly hit by the pandemic. The *Economist*, on the front cover of its 23 May 2020 issue, says, 'Seize the moment—the chance to flatten the climate curve'. Influential papers have asked for governments to enact policies to steer the economy away from carbon at lower financial, social, and political costs. One reason is the rock-bottom price of fossil fuel, making it sensible for government to remove subsidies, including carbon pricing schemes. The *Economist* reminds its readers that harm from climate change will be slower than the pandemic but more massive and longer lasting.

Business Commitments

Sustainability has become a part of business language and has helped reposition brand image to stay competitive and relevant. It is no longer enough to state the obvious reason of being more competitive and energy efficient. A strategy is needed to create value in the context of business, environment, and social performance.

By aligning sustainability philosophy and principles with their business strategies, companies have successfully gained efficiency and better brand image by going green across their business model, including distribution and supply chain. Members of the influential Climate Group, whose vision statement is 'A world of no more than 1.5 °C of global warming and greater prosperity for all', includes an network of global companies such as Apple, Kohl's, Google, Microsoft, Novo Nordisk, and Walmart. These companies have all made commitments and efforts to be climate neutral through elimination of waste, reliance on renewable energy, and sourcing of organic materials. The adoption of these principles is in line with one of their goals, which is to innovate solutions through sustainability. The success of this is seen in the case of large multinationals such as Unilever, which has put effort into recycling its waste and using environmental green standards in its production. Research efforts to minimise carbon footprints were reported in global carmakers' development of electric cars.

The convergence of technologies and sustainability principles will continue to produce an endless list of changes that aim to achieve sustainability goals. Businesses know that having a sustainability practice is important. The challenge is for them to continue translating mission statements into actions and pledges into tangible outcomes. According to the McKinsey & Company survey, companies that are actively integrating sustainability principles into their businesses capture better value through growth and returns on capital. These actions include enhancement of reputation through saving energy, developing green products, and retaining and motivating employees.

Consumers' Behaviours

Sustainability in the future cannot afford to ignore consumers' habits and attitudes as an important part of stakeholder change management. Bending the climate change curve demands more than an emphasis on clean technology. It must move away from a tried and tested linear economy to a circular economy. Decades of economic growth and development have utilised the earth's resources at an exponential rate, and this has led not only to resource depletion and pollution but also to an increase in the production of waste.

Society must be reminded to use resources not only responsibly but also sustainably. This requires a shift from the throwaway or waste culture towards a more sustainable one that involves buying what is necessary, reducing excessive consumption, recycling wherever possible, and going for more energy-efficient appliances.

Much progress has been made towards a ban on single-use plastic, but there have also been improvements on energy efficiency and substitution of low-carbon energy. Yet the percentage of waste being recycled continues to be low. Much has ended up in landfills, which brings a different set of challenges and problems. It is well known that 90 per cent of all litter that ends up in oceans is plastic. Packaging and consumables form the largest amount of waste items found floating in oceans, on beaches, or at the bottom of ocean floors. The drive towards such recycling is part of a circular economy where much waste material is recycled and reused for other purposes.

In reality, changing lifestyles can be extremely tricky and difficult, especially in a throwaway society, and to change their habits, consumers will need education and alternatives, including incentives or even deterrents. There is growing evidence that more consumers are conscious of what they shop for or use. This indicates that environmental issues do matter. It appears that, in the age of rising food and fuel prices, ethical consumerism continues to grow stronger. The market for energy-efficient appliances is also expected to grow in line with a conscious move to reduce the carbon footprint.

Future

The pandemic has demonstrated once again the need for more coherent global leadership and cooperation if the aspirations and goals of sustainability are ever to be realised. The United Nations is fully committed; despite the long process and hiccups, there are good reasons to believe the transition to realise its SDGs is in progress. While the rate of that progress may not be smooth, the pandemic experience has shown that such a sheer scale of global threat requires time and resources. The poorest and most vulnerable nations cannot be expected to bear the brunt of any of these global threats to their response system.

The sustainable future depends first and foremost on scientific and technological innovations to ensure a break from the addiction to high-carbon energy. The SDGs 2030 agenda echoed the crucial contribution of science and technology as powerful agents of change. But a sustainable future can be realised only when such innovations are accessible in price, convenience, and relevance. Rapid technological advances in energy systems are already here.

The future envisioned in *The Uninhabitable Earth* by David Wallace-Wells is still possible. According to him, if anything can save the planet, it will be technology. This includes electric cars, solar-powered energy systems, artificial intelligence, robotics, and biotechnologies. Equally important is political will and commitment. Trillions of dollars have been committed towards the deployment of clean technology for both advanced and developing countries.

Fresh opportunities to achieve the limits of global temperature rise of under 2 per cent now await from the economic stimulus packages announced by many governments in their efforts to avert economic downturn. The governments know that a new normal cannot return to conditions that promote forest fires, ecological damage, hunger, and social deprivation of food, water, and shelter.

The future of sustainability offers no other alternative but a low-carbon infrastructure. Shaping the future of sustainability requires the combined efforts of governments and their host of partners and civil societies. The best hope remains with them, as they have at their disposal the resources, influence, and mandate which they have promised but have not yet delivered.

CHAPTER 2

Denials

The issues and dangers surrounding climate change are not new. They have been making headlines for the past decade because scientists have made the adverse impacts of climate change on humanity more convincing with their evidence-based data. Indeed, for the past two decades, the weather patterns in many parts of the world have become more violent, unpredictable, and complex. Evidence of severe floods and forest fires are enough to make headlines, but it is debatable whether real action is taken once the situation returns to normal.

Global warming is no longer a scientific concept. Neither is it a recent discovery. Despite this, there is still the unfinished business of convincing a broad range of stakeholders who continue to deny that climate change exists. One of them is US President Donald Trump, who described climate change as a 'hoax' when he announced US withdrawal from the Paris climate agreement on 1 June 2017. Indeed, the US president, three years after his presidential election victory, was consistent as a climate sceptic; at the 2020 World

Economic Forum (WEF), he again derided climate change as a 'prophet of doom' in a speech and in a conference where the main theme was sustainability.

The US president is not alone. There are many who, for obvious economic and political reasons, choose not to listen to scientific evidence that climate change is human-induced and therefore real, and that changes to weather patterns can either bring excessive rain or none, leading to adverse conditions that could paralyse the entire business or community lifeline.

Shifting such a paradigm has been very time-consuming, let alone the need to convince policymakers and business leaders that global warming matters and that neglecting ecological matters will leave many economies and society paralysed by massive disruption. The scale of such destruction can be worse than what was experienced during the peak of the Covid-19 pandemic.

Climate change is already taking place, according to hard evidence from various scientific reports. Perhaps in the minds of the sceptics, the urgency to address it is not there. The unwillingness of many of these sceptics has to be accepted as one of the challenges to sustainability. There are many reasons why people continue to deny the existence of climate change.

Threats

A low-carbon economy poses an immediate threat to the fossil fuel industry. Billions have been spent on upstream activities and infrastructures, and the extraction industry has also moved on petrochemical businesses, all of which have been blamed for excessive carbon emissions over the decades, especially in advanced and emerging markets. It is not uncommon for such established industries to spend billions in lobbying for political support to ensure that they continue to receive favourable fiscal treatments and that they remain competitive against alternative renewable energy supply.

The fossil fuel supporters are also being accused of misleading the public with their public relations and community campaigns. The intent has always been to ensure public opinion remains neutral and supportive of the high-carbon lifestyle. Climate denial persists amongst some political and industry leaders who have publicly cast doubts on the scientific evidence on climate change. Climate change denial is not confined to a few such individuals. There are campaigns to cast doubt over climate evidence, with strong machinery to pursue specific economic interests and political ideology, supported by bloggers and fake news, all with the intention of creating uncertainty over the dangers of global warming.

Such scepticism is often linked to fossil fuels industry, and one could recall similar campaigns against antismoking efforts in the seventies. Business leaders are aware of the adverse consequences of climate change. *InsideClimate News*, the *Los Angeles Times*, and the Columbia Graduate School of Journalism reported the case of ExxonMobil, which made billions annually while at the same being aware of the dangers of climate change since the 1970s. The news led to thousands urging investigation of and litigation against the oil multinational. The event reaffirmed the business's continuing denial in favour of its pursuit of commercial interests.

For decades, the petroleum industry has led and supported the growth and development of economic infrastructure, including manufacturing and an entire supply chain of supporting industries and services. The automobile and airline industries are classic examples of such industries that have prospered during the peak of the fossil fuel era. The petroleum industry is often well supported by its own host government, through a broad range of subsides and fiscal measures. One recent example is the decision of the Australian federal government to offer subsidies to natural gas and oil refinery industries as part of its post pandemic economic recovery plan. Although experts believe the future of Australia energy policy rests with renewables, it is clear that heavy dependence on fossil fuel industry is far from over.

The adverse impacts on business performance are acknowledged across the broader spectrum of economic, environmental, and cultural dimensions. It is almost impossible to divorce the influence of business from its impacts on society. At the same time, the world has been reminded by concerned institutions—including the United Nations multilateral agencies, trade bodies, and regional bodies—that businesses should be doing greater good and providing greater transparency, more disclosures, and increased social responsibility.

Doing More

Businesses big and small are being reminded that they need to do more than just fulfil their commercial purpose. They have a social responsibility towards the communities they serve. There are already hundreds of large companies that have made this not only a mission statement but a way they are measured and judged. Impacts of climate change are acknowledged as risks and a material issue to the extent that the International Accounting Standards Board (IASB) has called for climate related risks be included in financial reporting.

There is no shortage of reminders to both international and local business leaders that businesses are accountable to the society in which they operate. The WEF attracts more than 3,000 influential and leading delegates from all over the world to its annual conference in Davos. For more than a decade, WEF has placed sustainability themes—including climate change, social inclusion, youth engagement, and technology disruptions—at the top of its conference agenda. Thousands of influential personalities have walked through the conference hall and meeting rooms in Davos, and it is not unreasonable to expect greater commitment to promoting the global agenda on sustainability, which ensures sustained growth and development.

Greenhouse Gas

The global problem of climate change is no stranger to the community of environmental scientists. The concept of the greenhouse effect was first noted by the European scientists way back in the nineteenth century. The United Nations hosted its first conference on the topic in Stockholm in 1972. Issues raised at the conference were confined to chemical pollution and possible dangers and threats of nuclear energy to peace and societies. The term *global warming* was first coined by Wallace Broecker, a US scientist, when he presented a paper at a scientific conference in 1975. It led to the formation of the Intergovernmental Panel on Climate Change (IPCC), whose purpose and role would be to collate and assess trends in carbon emission and its impacts on climate change.

Perhaps the most significant piece of research to be published has been the Stern Review in October 2006. Written by leading economist Sir Nicholas Stern, the report on the economics of climate change examined the 'business as usual (BAU)' scenario and 'strong, early action' scenario in terms of costs and benefits.

The results of the study show a strong case for acting now. Stern estimated that BAU would incur a 5 to 10 per cent loss of global GDP, with this being as much as to 10 per cent in poor countries. When considering other issues, such as impact on the environment and human health, the total estimated cost of climate change would lead to a 20 per cent reduction in consumption per head. Aside from the cost, if nothing was done, the projected temperature would be expected to rise by 5 to 6 °C, taking the world into uncharted territory never experienced by humans before. Alternatively, taking some immediate drastic action to stabilise carbon emissions by 2050 was estimated to come at a cost of around 1 per cent of GDP, significantly less than the BAU scenario. Now, more than ten years since the report, it remains to be seen whether the long-term investments in renewable energy and energy efficiency recommended by Stern have been put into place.

Beyond Profits

Today, the expectations for business in society have gone beyond profits and wealth. To an extent, global businesses are better informed as to how their business should be conducted and perceived of, at least from the climate-risk perspective. Undoubtedly, more and more attention is given to the potential implications and impact on the local environment and surrounding areas. Thanks to the influence of social media on how business performance shapes and influence societal values, expectations and attitudes are constantly being raised, especially from the compliance and risk perspectives.

Values

Although business history will not ignore the developments of climate change awareness among a wide range of stakeholders that includes consumers, employees, investors, communities, and governments, we now share common beliefs due to a convergence of universal values that cut across national boundaries. The initial accusation that climate change is a Western thing will increasingly diminish. Thanks to social media, many stakeholders are expecting local actions to be taken to overcome the problems of climate change.

While customers will still want higher standards of service and value for money, they too are receptive to, say, a no-plastic campaign or recycling being made mainstream. Shareholders too will still want greater returns, but no longer can this be achieved at the expense of the fragile environment and public interest.

Public Awareness

A 2015 online survey from forty countries shows that climate change does matter to a majority of locals. In the vast majority of countries, less than 3 per cent said climate change was not important or serious. The research by the University of Oxford's Reuters Institute in its annual Digital News Reports also showed differences in perceptions among diverse geographies. But the overall trend was that concern for climate change was rising, even in the United States, where two in three said they were 'somewhat' worried about global warming. This was a vast improvement in a country which has one of the highest carbon footprints.

Indeed, it was not until the release of *An Inconvenient Truth*, a documentary that highlighted global warming and the dangerous repercussions of carbon emissions to the economies and societies, that awareness in the United States began to rise. Featuring former US vice president Al Gore as its main narrator, the award-winning documentary has been praised for raising public awareness of global warming, but it also accelerated an increase in the number of businesses and companies committed towards going green through a drastic improvement in fuel efficiency and embracing more environmentally friendly practices. It convinced a higher percentage of Americans that global warming caused by human activities was harmful, according to the Pew Research Centre.

Climate Activism

Campaigns against fossil fuel attracted an unlikely ally in Greta Thunberg. Famous for saying 'How dare you, you have stolen my dreams and my childhood with your empty words' in front of world leaders at the 2019 UN climate action summit, she represents one of the new and young generation campaigning for real action against climate change. The voice of the younger generation has now grown louder and attracted more attention. Even the WEF has not lose sight of this trend. Elsewhere, the *New York Times* reported on 17 January 2020 that a lawsuit against the state in United States for climate change was thrown out. It would have been a landmark case.

Scientific Truth

The overwhelming evidence produced by the scientific, environmental, and economic communities leave few people in doubt that climate change is happening, albeit gradually, and that it poses a potentially serious threat to humanity. If global temperatures continue to rise at the same rate as in recent years, then soon, there will be severe consequences for both developed and developing countries. *Time* magazine produced special edition on global warming way back in 2012 which considered the case on such climate change as closed. *Time* agreed with the scientists' argument that excessive 'emission of greenhouse gases like carbon dioxide fossil fuels, like coal or oil, and those gases are burnt and collected in the atmosphere would warm the planet'.

It is scientists, after all, who monitored, analysed, and produced the report and data which regulators and governments must use to assess standing policy in the short and long term. It is scientists who have the expertise to contribute to public policy and research on climate and environmental challenges and goals. There is no shortage of reliable big data from multiple sources that policymakers will be able to act on for both business and social implications. They can put forward a broad range of instruments—including taxes, subsidies and incentives—across the economies. Indeed, the potential of available intelligence has given sustainability champions the opportunity to pursue more rigorous goals including reporting of risks and developments.

There are many roles people can or should play to make a difference in the global understanding of climate change. Governments are key to managing the politics of climate change. They can and must make environmental considerations and development policy a top priority. Consumers can try to make informed choices about what environmentally friendly products they should buy and what resources they really need. The business community can reduce waste and work to measure and control the pollution that it inflicts on the environment. These are contributions, but not enough to make an impact.

Government

Governments must be at the forefront in championing the sustainability agenda. The implications of climate change, if not addressed, are widespread and pose serious and direct threats not only to the global economy and environment but to the basic elements essential for life. The most basic of these is a reliable supply of water and food resources, which is clearly vulnerable to climate change.

For example, a slight increase in temperature in mountainous regions will accelerate the rate of the melting of glaciers. This, in turn, will increase the risk of flooding and seriously deplete long-term water supplies, predominantly affecting low-lying communities in the Indian subcontinent, parts of China, and low-lying areas of the Americas. The loss of a sustainable source of water, such as a glacier which feeds irrigating rivers, will lead to a decline in crops, with serious implications for communities whose livelihoods and food supplies depend on agriculture. Recent statistics show that increased carbon emissions have raised the global temperature by 0.5 °C, and the world is the hottest it has been in 12,000 years,

Although these potentially very serious changes are likely to eventually affect countries all around the world, it is those communities which are least equipped with the capacity to deal with them, both economically and structurally, that will be hit first and hardest. The Covid-19 pandemic demonstrated the weakness of healthcare systems to cope with large-scale disaster. It is the developing world that will be expected to struggle to cope with extreme climates. Developing countries and communities are, by nature, more dependent on agriculture, which is vulnerable to increasing temperatures or flooding, leading to increased poverty and an inability to be self-sustaining.

A host of related problems awaits each of these disasters waiting to happen. Economic denial is hard to ignore in oil-exporting nations, where 90 per cent of export revenue relies on petroleum products. Heavy dependence on such revenue has led many of these governments to ignore opportunities to diversify to green technologies. Global exports of oil and gas are worth trillions among the top oil-exporting countries. Given the size of opportunity cost, not many will be prepared to give up their golden eggs. It is obvious the gradual shift to renewable energy will not serve their economic interests including the large gas producing nations, not now or the near future.

International Efforts

Several initiatives, treaties, coalitions, and reports have been created and written over the last few decades to identify the best ways to share responsibility among global leaders in the effort to combat the effects of climate change. From the creation of a carbon market to an endless list of mitigating efforts led by the United Nations agencies, ensuring a consistent and fair international policy and treaties on mitigation of climate change is not easy.

There have been several important conventions since the significant milestone of the 1997 Kyoto Protocol, which as an international treaty extended commitments among participating nations to reduce greenhouse gas emission. Since Kyoto, several conventions have taken place. At the Paris climate convention in 2015, the 187 member countries agreed to keep long-term global warming to no more than 2 per cent above preindustrial levels and to limit the increase to 1.5 °C by the year 2030, by far the most significant commitment so far. The general view is that much needs to be done to succeed with such goals. If they do succeed, the risks and impacts of climate change would be reduced.

Responsibility

Protecting the planet and its natural resources is a responsibility and a concern which calls upon all to consider how global leaders can do their part despite of their vested economic interests in protecting their bread and butter. Governments come and go, but they can play a role as saviours of the planet. Failure to do so is not an option. Each government has its responsibility to fulfil. Denial is not an answer.

CHAPTER 3

Politics

The climate emergency summit in Melbourne in February 2020 declared officially that the warming earth was a threat to Australian society and civilisation. The declaration was made in the wake of Australia's worst-ever bush fire, which destroyed more than 110,000 square kilometres and killed thirty-three humans and millions of wildlife. The summit, according to the *Guardian*, concluded that the global climate had reached a dangerous level in all continents and the earth had become unacceptably hot. The summit jointly declared the following:

> If the climate warms 1.5 °C above pre-industrial levels, the Great Barrier Reef will likely be lost, sea levels could rise metres and massive global carbon stores such as the Amazon and Greenland, will hit tipping points, releasing millions of tonnes of carbon into the atmosphere.

Such declaration is not the first, and neither will it be the last. The unprecedented Australian fire has invoked much emotion around the country as well as around the world. But it is questionable whether it will have a long-term effect on public opinion and, importantly, politics and government.

Political Differences

Political leaders of countries such as the United States and Brazil are not taking the same stand on climate change repercussions. Clearly, the decision of the US government to withdraw from the 2016 Paris Agreement on climate has been significant. It merely tells the extent of political challenges.

Understandably, the politics of climate changes are complex, taking into consideration the economics of interest groups that will not be easy to tackle. The withdrawal of US leadership in climate treaties has left a huge gap, and the implication could even lead to others following in the footsteps of the United States. President Trump has made it clear that he does not wish US to be bound by the principles and agreement made at Paris in 2016.

Adverse Consequences

Many experts have agreed that any increase above the 2° C threshold on global warming would bring adverse consequences. Poorer countries would be hardest hit, especially those with low-lying geographies. They would experience the extremes of weather, from frequent floods to prolonged drought. Either would pose potential threats to food security.

It is predicted that the scale of the damage to earth's ecological stability will be unthinkable. Consequences that can be expected include social chaos and political instability in the most fragile societies as soon as the system that holds everything together breaks down. A wave of climate migrants will emerge as thousands seek safer ground in search of survival.

The problem of climate crisis is acknowledged as one of the biggest global challenges. It has been acknowledged among influential business leaders at the annual World Economic Forum (WEF) that climate change must be recognised and addressed. Among the many who are committed to comprehensive action is Jeff Bezos, the world's richest man. According to a Reuters report, the Amazon owner has, on 17 February 2020, committed USD 10 billion to fund scientists, non-profits, and activist groups to protect the environment from climate change.

Challenges

Climate change is already a political mainstream issue at international, regional, and local levels. A broad United Nations framework for policymakers offering a coherent road map on how national governments should go about forming long-term carbon emission policies has already been made known. Therein lie the challenges of political will and implementation.

The level of public awareness and frequency of discussion of climate change has increased over time. Many of these debates, from the highest level to the grassroots, receive media attention. There is already much scientific evidence that climate change is real and happening, from unusual weather patterns to economic and social impacts. These developments have given rise to the establishment of international frameworks and agreements, including carbon trading and funding, technological research and innovation, and more recently, the agreement to cap the rise in carbon emissions to no more than 2 °C by the year 2030.

Priorities

But the UN commitment on climate change only tells part of the story. None of the advanced members have fulfilled the promises and commitments made at each of the climate summits, based on scientific reports on carbon emissions every year. The commitments for better performance, governance, and accountability have shifted to the responsibilities of national governments towards the nonbinding international treaties on carbon emissions and financial support for the protection of environment and society in the least developed nations.

There has been more attention focused on adaptation measures and actions. There has been no shortage of ideas being advocated and proposed to government leaders and regulators. There are governments that have embraced these as national commitments, where they can become an integral part of UN's sustainable development goals (SDGs). Indeed, such goals have been re-emphasised at various high-level climate conferences and political meetings.

The call for global duties—that is, fulfilling global targets—has been both challenging and complex. The relatively small number of countries committed to massive reduction of carbon and the lip service among a few national leaders are bad news for staunch climate advocates. Ensuring countries go beyond commitments requires more than persuasion. While public opinion may help to convince governments in Western democracies, others generally need to be convinced that international commitment will serve their national interest. Enabling national and local policies will depend on national leadership where it matters.

Such challenges, at a national level, are not hard to ascertain. Many governments see reduction of the global carbon footprint as the responsibility of rich nations, typically the European Union, Japan, United States, United Kingdom, Canada, Australia, and even China. There is no shortage of awareness activities on reasons and priorities for the reduction in carbon emission. At the local level, climate sceptics continue to doubt whether direct government intervention is necessary, especially when it involves substituting the fossil fuel-driven economies with lesser-known technologies. This and the perception that renewable energy costs are higher are often the main reasons behind the lack of urgency.

Fossil Fuel

Many countries continue to rely heavily on fossil fuel to drive their economic activities. The cheaper option of using coal is common, and this is easily accessible. Fossil fuel energy is generally used to support industry, agriculture, transport, and households. Coal-fired power plants are the biggest generator of CO_2, and although consumption patterns have been in decline in Europe and the United States, both China and India remain significant users.

Australia, too, has been blamed as a net contributor to rising carbon emissions because coal has been a major export revenue. Indeed, the politics of climate change has posed a massive political dilemma for the Australian government. Successive governments do recognise that coal exports are worth USD 15 billion annually, yet the people are increasingly aware of the threat global warming has posed to the nation's ecology, communities, and people. The recent case of the protests of the mining giant Adani building the biggest coal mine in its state of Queensland has pushed the politics of climate change even further out to the forefront.

China, as the world's leader in manufacturing, relies on cheap coal as its main energy source to fuel every single part of its global supply chain of production and delivery. The government in China has committed to reduction of CO_2, and the country is also devoted to development and deployment of new technology in hydroelectric and solar to substitute for coal. These strategies would require time, and time is something the world may not have.

While there is evidence of governments phasing out coal-fired power plants in Europe, in Japan there has been a disturbing report that the country is leaning towards coal power. The *New York Times* reported that a total of twenty-two coal-fired power plants may be added to Japan's seventeen sites over the next five years. This is enough to add a total of 75 million tonnes of CO_2 annually. Under the Paris Agreement, Japan is committed to reduce its 2013 figure of 26 per cent by 2030. Politically, the government is committed to become carbon neutral after 2050. Its Tokyo Olympic Games, postponed to 2021, are meant to be carbon neutral, but the government's energy policy is obviously opposed to its strategy of becoming a carbon neutral.

It is expected that fossil fuel demand will continue to rise to fuel economic growth in the countries of South East Asia. Realistically, dependence on the cheaper source of energy, coal, and the recent drop in the price of oil and gas reinforces the complacency. Access to renewable energy technologies—especially solar, hydro and even wind—to complement heavy dependence on fossil fuel remains less of a priority. Without access to low-carbon technology and assurance of its reliability, it would be quite a challenge for many emerging countries to move away from their dependence on fossil fuel so soon and become net contributors to CO_2 reduction.

At the international level, the climate change agenda has moved from awareness and sharing of its adverse effects to one that binds nations together in a common set of goals and targets reduction and mitigating actions. The agreement of nations to cooperate on an international scale was first made at the 2010 UN Climate Change Conference in Cancun. The Paris summit in 2016 saw a historic agreement among nations to keep the global temperature warming this century to no more than 2 °C and a broad framework allowing new technology and capacity-building to support developing nations.

Diverse Interests

The absence of US leadership from the UN climate treaties demonstrates the complexity of the situation and the huge challenge of having all nations drive the agenda in one common direction. The United States, under a previous regime, had rejected the Kyoto proposal back in 2005. The current president, Donald Trump, has made it clear that his government does not wish to be involved in the UN-backed climate change initiative. Instead, he has agreed to the proposal of planting one trillion trees. By his estimate, tree planting could eliminate eight or nine years of recent CO_2 emission. Critics have warned that while such a greening effort of the planet is welcomed, it is not sufficient, as such an idea is impractical and problematic in implementation.

At the international level, it is hard to get countries to agree on the obligations made in the Paris climate accord in 2016. There are outcomes to be ironed out at the Glasgow meeting in 2021. Much needs to be done with regards to technicalities in the carbon market. In the final analysis, nations continue to press on for final dollars and cents to assist in their obligations.

There are also the challenges of defining responsibilities, as commitments made are nonbinding. Brazil, for example, was a global leader at the climate conference in Paris in 2016. But this has changed, as the Jair Bolsonaro government wants to move away from clean energy and expand its carbon footprint through massive clearing of the Amazon rainforest. According to the National Institute for Space Research, Amazon forests no longer have the capacity to produce 20 per cent of the earth's oxygen. The new administration does not see this as its moral obligation; rather, the Amazon forest is be exploited for its rich wealth of copper, gold, nickel, and other resources.

There are, too, climate sceptics including fossil fuel industry that have remain doubtful as to whether the environment should be given emphasis and priority. This gives policymakers plenty of excuses not to pursue a more rigorous approach. The lack of understanding amongst policymakers, coupled with industry lobbies, has also prevented several environmental-based policies from getting through. Complaints from proenvironmental groups are not uncommon, which makes it even harder for local laws to be introduced. Indeed, climate issues are now commonly debated in parliaments as well as political parties.

The *Guardian* reported in December 2019 on a landmark case in the Netherlands, where the supreme court ordered the government to cut more carbon emissions to protect its citizens. Such cases are the exception rather than the norm. A keen supporter of the climate change movement, former UN High Commissioner Mary Robinson, has said that 'the denial of climate change is not just ignorant, but malign and evil because it denies the human rights of the most vulnerable people on the planet'. In this context, she echoed the view that fossil fuel companies have lost their social license to operate, and these companies must transit to clean and renewable energy.

Low-Carbon Investment

After enduring a summer of intense heat waves, bush fires, drought, floods, and storms, Australians are increasingly aware of the threat global heating poses to our way of life. But as leading scientists race to solve the climate crisis, they face the challenge of having to compete with investment opportunities. For example, the proposition offered by mining giant Adani to build the biggest coal mine in state of Queensland provoked a state-wide protest arguing the proposed coal mine would pose a threat to the ancestral lands, water sources, and cultures of its indigenous people, put a precious reserve of groundwater at risk, and add 4.6 billion tonnes of carbon pollution to the global atmosphere.

Elsewhere, there are governments committed to developing low-emission zones. The Singapore government, for example, allocated SGD 5 billion to its coastal and flood protection fund to build infrastructure to tackle the risk of rising sea levels. The government recognised the challenge to reduce its carbon footprint through a green towns programme comprising of reduction in energy consumption, recycling of rainwater, and cooling of the environment.

Despite all the odds, member states of the United Nations have made their commitment to the goal of a 2 per cent increase in carbon emissions by the year 2030. The fact that these commitments are not legally binding makes it difficult for scientists to remain assured or convinced. At the biannual UN climate convention, there was strong evidence of a massive gap in expectations between wealthy and poorer nations. The debate has centred on the question of who pays and how much. There is also a moral argument that those who consumed most should be the ones to sponsor the most in both financing of technology and commitment towards reduction of carbon emissions.

Enforcement

Governments in both advanced and emerging markets often have to deal with the political challenge of penalising those with bigger carbon footprints—for example, motorists. Governments face political backlash if the penalties are above the motorists' limits. Such protests were seen in Germany, France, and even Chile. Any increase in fuel may also provoke protests from groups acting on behalf of the poor or pensioners, who will be the first to bear the brunt of any inflation of fuel prices.

A switch towards low-carbon economies based on fiscal policies will not be easy, as often the ones to suffer are the poorer segments of society. This is why it is often hard for any populist government to remove subsidies, for example from petroleum products. This hinders any plan to raise the price of fossil fuel. Dropping the climate agenda is convenient and easier for any populist government eager to win political office.

If affordable pricing continues to be one of the main issues, then a gradual reduction in the price of renewable energy will help remove one of the obstacles. Indeed, the spin-off effects on other aspects of the economy may be positive. But such assumptions may not be accurate. The climate change issue is complex and requires collective solutions, but years of negotiation at the highest political levels remained unresolved and unclear. Even the voluntary commitments made at the Paris meeting in 2016 have not necessarily led to concrete solutions, as seen at the Madrid meeting in 2019.

There will always be a diverse group of parties pursuing their own political and commercial agenda. The politics of climate change cannot ignore the strong campaign and lobbying efforts of the huge oil and gas companies. Apart from the multinationals like ExxonMobil, BP, or Shell, there are hundreds of state-owned petroleum-based companies. These companies have spent billions in their campaigns to protect their market share as well as justify the need for subsidies for developmental purposes. Lobbying their respective governments is a common way to protect their leadership position. These companies have a big say in energy consumption. Indeed, many continue to lobby for more financial support towards extracting new sources of supply.

Although civil societies have campaigned for green energy, they too will need to win political support. There is now a need for these parties to use public opinion as part of their influential strategy. Lobbying for or against climate change policies will intensify as the year to realise the SDGs get closer. There will be winners and losers, but one for sure, with which not many will disagree, is that the earth will get hotter, and for the ambitious targets of SDGs to be realised, politics have to be tackled first.

CHAPTER 4

Justice

On 24 September 2019, Greta Thunberg and fifteen other young people caught the world's attention by filing a legal suit against five countries: Argentina, Brazil, France, Germany, and Turkey. These are the countries alleged to have the largest carbon footprint.

Climate Activism

Greta Thunberg gained overnight recognition by speaking up on climate change in front of influential and prominent political and business leaders. She on several occasions was applauded for speaking up on the dangers of climate change to the world leaders and accusing them of not doing enough to tackle the global concerns of climate change. At the 2019 United Nations General Assembly meeting, she said, shaking with rage:

> This is all wrong, I shouldn't be up here. I should be back in school on the other side of the ocean. You have stolen my dreams, my

childhood with your empty words. We will
not let you get away with this. Right here,
right now is where we draw the line.

Her complaint as a climate activist will be heard by a committee of eighteen international human rights experts. According to the United Nations Foundations, the committee will need to study the complaint and make its own recommendations to all parties in a process which can take up to two years. A favourable outcome can provide a symbolic victory that includes a reinforcement of the countries' obligations agreed at the Paris climate agreement.

Climate Justice

The *Guardian* on 4 July 2019 reported that climate action lawsuits against governments and corporations have taken place in at least twenty-eight countries. The newspaper reported a study showed more than 1,300 legal actions concerning climate change had been recorded in the past two decades. In terms of country breakdown, the United States leads in climate litigation, whilst in other countries there has been increase in cases involving individuals versus the state. In the Netherlands, there was a case where the court ruled in favour of young people who sued the government for doing nothing on climate change. There have been examples of climate litigation cases even in Colombia and Pakistan.

Climate justice is a term used to frame global warming in an ethical and social context, rather than one that is purely environmental or physical in nature. This is done by relating the effects of climate change to concepts of justice, particularly the impacts on societies and people. Such environmental and social justice issues are addressed in a social context and related to such issues as equality, human rights, and collective rights. Complaints are often based on the principles of responsibility and public accountability.

An important consideration related to climate justice is that those who are least responsible for climate change suffer its gravest consequences. Climate justice represents one of the biggest challenges of the twenty-first century, as such a reaction to seek justice for climate change not only addresses the concept of social equity but is also about highlighting the inequality and unfairness of who bears the worst consequences of climate change across countries and people. Climate justice is also seen as a movement built on the principles of social justice to address the environmental impact on disadvantaged groups, allowing them an opportunity to gain social equity and fairness.

The term *climate justice* is also used to mean actual legal action on climate change issues. In 2017, a report of the United Nations Environment Programme identified 894 ongoing legal actions worldwide. There have occasionally been public protests on climate change. Environmental protests on a large scale have taken place in cities such as New York and, more recently, London.

Wikipedia refers to climate justice as legal action to address climate change issues. The United Nations Environment Programme (UNEP) in 2017 reported that there is a rough estimate of nine hundred ongoing legal cases worldwide. Climate justice can be seen from an ethical and fairness perspective. There are climate change movements that see climate justice as a way to express their human rights and collective rights to represent society in a way that will make the government take notice.

Climate justice today is not just one green thing but a serious social movement that focuses on human right, equal rights, and fair treatment irrespective of ethnicity. Climate justice rests on the principle that everyone is entitled to fresh air, clean water, and protection from the harmful effects of chemicals and toxic fumes.

The concept of climate justice has gained momentum over the past decade, although it has not yet covered the globe. In many advanced markets, climate justice can be seen from environmental and justice perspectives. It is also being seen as a community issue, as any changes in climate would most hurt the bottom 40 per cent of the population, as lower socio-economic groups are typically the most exposed and vulnerable to the effects of climate change and would receive the brunt of the negative effects.

Indeed, the World Bank has officially forecast that the earth is on track for a warmer climate—as much as 4 degrees hotter, which would translate into volatile weather across different continents, where there would be prolonged droughts that would directly threaten the earth's ecosystem and food security.

Politics

Climate issues can become emotional, appealing especially to younger segments of the population. They draw attention especially in a world that has increasingly become more polarised between the haves and have nots. Recent trends in Western democracies have seen issues surrounding sustainability gaining more popular support. Climate justice has also become an electoral issue in some of the more recent general elections in advanced democracies.

Climate issues have become, in some cases, an electoral pledge by candidates wanting to gain votes. Often, election pledges come in the form of what they would do in the adaptation process, as well with access to resources to address the effects of climate change, should they win and gain political power. The Green Party does not command majority popular support to form a government in most democracies. But their voicing of issues on waste, ecology degradation, social deprivation, and climate-related matters often push the main parties to take a position. In a way, green issues can be appealing to voters, especially in marginal seats.

Sustainability matters have also gone beyond the main policies. In the United States, for example, the Republican-controlled federal government would not be able to stop states and cities from adopting the Paris climate accord and principles.

Visual Impact

The way climate issues have affected local communities was illustrated in the documentary *Paris to Pittsburgh*—a film produced by Bloomberg Philanthropies and RadicalMedia and distributed by National Geographic Documentary Films. The title of the documentary was based on a phrase used by President Trump on 1 June 2017 when he proudly announced the withdrawal of the United States from the Paris climate agreement and added, 'I was elected to represent the citizens of Pittsburgh, not Paris'. In response, Bill Peduto, mayor of Pittsburgh, wrote: 'As the Mayor of Pittsburgh, I can assure you that we will follow the guidelines of the Paris Agreement for our people, our economy and future'.

Greenpeace sees such documentaries as bringing to light the impassioned efforts of individuals who are battling the most severe threats of climate change in their own backyards. The documentary was written against the real national debate over US energy policies and their effect on the environment.

It sends an important message about what is at stake for local communities around the country—and the inspiring ways Americans are responding.

The increasing interest and attention on climate justice is equally driven by the realisation and recognition of the impact climate change has on local economies. For example, years of rising sea levels in Miami resulting from climate change provoked a headline that appears in the 2 May 2018 *Guardian*: 'Everglades under threat as Florida's mangroves face death by rising sea level'.

Scientists warned local government of the rising sea level that has intruded inland into Everglades National Park, which is home to many rare and endangered plants, such as tropical orchids and herbs, as well as important parts of the entire ecosystem. Rising sea waters would increase salinity, and that is not good news to local communities and surrounding ecosystems that depend on water for economic and social needs. For years now, these parks in south Florida have struggled to reverse the damage that failure to directly address the problems posed by climate change have brought about. Local politicians in communities will now need to understand and allocate enough funds to mitigate climate change adaptation.

For climate justice to be served, it must overcome politics and legal challenges. While collectivism and movement help resilience and momentum, they depend on resources as well as political will and support. Leadership is important, as well as legal support that individuals, groups, and civil societies can rely on. Even Greta Thunberg will discover that overcoming the politics of climate change demands more than just a strong airing of the truth at the highest platform. Sustainability needs to be self-reliant and overcome a complexity of variables and political constraints at every level.

CHAPTER 5

Challenges

The prevailing Covid-19 pandemic has wreaked havoc across the global economy and community. The virus has rapidly infected more than 30 million people across more than 215 countries, causing more than 900,000 deaths as of September 2020. According to the World Health Organisation (WHO), the mortality rate as of April 2020 was 3.4 per cent but rising, as the disease has no vaccine and infection spreads easily through close human contact, posing a major risk to sensitive economies and fragile societies across the planet.

Global Risks

Covid-19 has proven deadly in developed markets like the United States, Spain, France, Germany, the United Kingdom, and Italy, where tens of thousands have been infected and thousands have died. Elsewhere, in India, Indonesia, Philippines, Brazil, and South Africa, the number infected remains on an upward trend. Despite a number of actions taken to confront the pandemic, it has been obvious that health systems are barely coping and are showing signs of risks and vulnerability.

A prolonged outbreak of the virus would, in the opinions of experts, affect the sustainability of the global supply chain, leaving tens of thousands of people facing an uncertain future. There will be severe consequences that put a strain on social systems and stability. The pandemic has, in a short period of time, proven to be the greatest threat to the vulnerability of public health and social stability in modern times.

Economic Impacts

Initial United Nations studies on the economic impact of the coronavirus pandemic estimated that the global economy would shrink by more than 3 per cent for the year 2020, but this meant millions of workers losing their jobs from the closure of thousands of business across all sectors.

As countries started closing their borders and big cities experienced a virtual lockdown in their effort to contain the infection, a rapid slowing down of the economy was inevitable. Although not all industries were directly hit, in an interconnected economy, a ripple effect throughout the global chain of activities would be expected. For example, businesses related to travel, hotel, tourism, retail services, and entertainment would be affected. The cascading effect throughout the dependencies includes loss of billions in revenue, and closure will even hit manufacturing and transportation. Global stock markets reacted negatively to the bad economic news, as investors were concerned over the broader economic implications of the pandemic.

The pandemic has made all economic planners return to the drawing board. Indeed, all governments were forced to dig deeper into their reserves to save jobs and get their local economies moving. Many central banks were asked to find ways and means to help industries that were financially affected while assisting consumers with their property loans to prevent an increase in foreclosures. There are equally thousands that have gone digital with their business continuity but there will be many that find it difficult to continue with the uncertainty.

With tighter border controls and an expected slowdown in economies, many countries are at the brink of a recession resulting from the rippling effects of a shutdown in the movement of activities across borders. Governments have introduced various stimulus budgets as part of the mitigating actions and plans.

Ecology

From an ecological perspective, there are researchers who view the outbreak of Covid-19 as a phenomenon that should have not been a surprise. The state of health on this planet has been constantly under threat for decades. There has been strong evidence of a fragile earth ecosystem at the brink of destruction, which has a serious impact on humanity and its ecosystem.

The troubled environment has resulted in loss of living ecosystems not only in the ocean but in the forests. Deforestation has been accelerating at an alarming rate. The Food and Agriculture Organisation 2016 State of the Forests report revealed a staggering 7 million hectares of virgin forests lost annually, mostly to agricultural activities and urbanisation.

The coronavirus outbreak, according to leading ecology experts, can be seen as an unintended consequence of the imbalance of the ecosystems. According to David Quammen, author of *Spillover: Animal Infections and the Next Pandemic*:

> We invade tropical forests and other wild landscapes, which harbour so many species of animals and plants – and within those creatures, so many unknown viruses ... We cut the trees; we kill the animals or cage them and send them to markets. We disrupt ecosystems, and we shake viruses loose from their natural hosts. When that happens, they need a new host. Often, we are it.

Similar accusation was raised during the outbreak of Ebola epidemics in Africa in the 1990s. It is well known among scientists that new diseases in humans, such as Ebola, SARS, H1N1 bird flu and now Covid-19, originated in animals. There are, however, leading scientists and medical experts who strongly believe that humanity's unending greed and the destruction of biodiversity have created the right conditions for new viruses and diseases to emerge.

Infections

Covid-19 is so infectious that it has been proven to have profound health and economic impacts in rich and poor countries alike. Indeed, no one can be blamed for thinking of a strong but obvious cause and effect of human consumption and treatment towards wildlife and entire ecosystems. The Chinese government has issued an immediate ban on trading and consumption of wildlife. The ban represents one of the immediate implications of the coronavirus that infected more 80,000 of the locals in Wuhan city.

The virus, although not proven to have, was thought to have originated from bats, which could have passed the virus to an intermediary species which then passed it to humans at the market in Wuhan. The *South China Morning Post* reported on 11 March 2020 that such wildlife trade has been estimated to be worth more than USD 74 billion, and a ban would not be easy to implement, as China's existing wildlife protection laws on conservation, trade, and consumption were enacted only in 1989 and contain loopholes. For example, consumption of wild animals and captive breeding was allowed for commercial purposes. The newspaper further reported that an epidemic such as severe acute respiratory syndrome or SARS was linked to consumption of civet cats, also in China, and this was confirmed by the WHO.

Many scientists regard animal-borne viruses as a real and significant threat to humanity, as well as both the health and security of any nation. The arrival of a global pandemic represents a wake-up call. Years of warnings of a possible collision between species as humans and animals compete for space and survival has put undue stress on the entire fragile ecosystem. The Covid-19 outbreak is just the beginning of the far-reaching consequences of such conflict. It is also the beginning of a series of risks, not only to sustainability development objectives but to all of humanity.

Positive Impacts

One area of the ecosystem that has been affected in a positive way is air quality, with a drastic decrease in levels of air pollutants and carbon emissions over most cities in advanced markets and regions. The main reason cited by the

BBC news on 19 March 2020 is a significant drop in air travel and transportation.

The BBC further reported that the sharp drop in emission of carbon was also due to a sharp drop in economic activities. A recent survey showed that in New York alone, the amount of carbon monoxide from cars was reduced by 50 per cent on a year-to-year comparison. Similar experiences were observed by studies done in Italy and China. Rob Jackson, chairman of the Global Carbon Project, which was responsible for monitoring and reporting annual emission estimates, said carbon output could fall by as much as 5 per cent, according to a Reuters report. Data from the Sentinel-5P satellite revealed air pollution levels of nitrogen dioxide decreased in Europe by as much as 20 to 30 per cent during the first week of the lockdown.

Climate scientists welcomed these positive changes that had not been predicted before the coronavirus pandemic. But this good news came with a sudden halt in economies, with more than a million people infected and thousands more losing their lives. The earth's gradual recovery may go unnoticed due to the sudden halt in human and economic activities. At any rate, the drop is regarded as only temporary relief.

Response and Limits

One significant repercussion of the coronavirus pandemic has been the proposed ban on wildlife trade and consumption announced by the Chinese government. The *Guardian* online reported on 9 April 2020 that the Chinese government had announced an end to human consumption of dogs and cats as part of the overall draft policy in response to growing public outcry over animal cruelty but significantly as a way to prevent disease transmission from animals to humans. China's Ministry of Agricultural and Rural Affairs has proposed to reclassify dog meat as not fit for human consumption. Already the city of Shenzhen has taken the first step to legislate against consumption of dog and cat meat, a move that animal welfare groups have given the thumbs-up.

These developments are significant, although the regulations will not eliminate the wildlife trade completely, as fashion businesses depends on procuring animal skins and furs for their finished products. With an industry valued at more than USD 70 billion, China is the largest source of fur and leather serving the advanced and emerging markets for luxury goods. Banning the trade completely would lead to an increase in illegal trafficking that goes under the radar of the authorities. The industry continues to enjoy phenomenal growth fuelled by world demand. Boston Consulting Group predicts the growth to be as high as 63 per cent in overall fashion consumption in the period from 2017 to 2030.

Rising consumerism has meant more and more people cannot resist buying clothes or fashion accessories made from natural animal skins or furs. Growing affluence coupled with rising fashion consciousness in both developed and emerging markets have meant that farms created for breeding animals from mink fox to ostriches to crocodiles will continue to thrive.

While China today is the world's largest producer of fur for the high-end clothing industry, there are equally others in South America and elsewhere to serve the demand mostly from the advanced markets. There are estimated to be more than 100 million animals involved; some are bred for their fur while others are captured in the wild and often skinned for their fur. There are limits, but placing an ethical element on such trade that involves cruelty to animals can help arouse consumer emotions.

Potential Risks

While the pandemic has brought about disruptions to both economic and social developments, there is optimism based on several significant but positive developments. The pandemic that has locked down major cities has also pushed many to go online and look at a business model which could accelerate the development of more activities going online. The adoption of new work processes and lifestyles would also allow renewable energy to catch up, although ironically, with fossil fuel prices dropping, this would not incentivise many to be bothered with the green agenda.

Importantly many governments could finally see the difference and act with the same urgency and commitment on climate. Leading scientists also believe the health pandemic has brought home a message on the importance of health as a public concern and as an important sustainability matter to be addressed across the seventeen SDGs.

CHAPTER 6

Opportunities

The immediate impact of high unemployment, especially amongst lower-income earners, is one that has kept political leaders anxious, especially in the United States, where business and economic barriers were removed prematurely, and for remaining markets that have flattened the curve. The opening of businesses and offices will come with a set of new of rules and guidelines that have to be complied with.

The BBC reported on 23 April 2020 that European Union leaders were planning to inject billions of euros of emergency aid into the battered economies of Europe. Elsewhere, there were similar stories. Fear of mass unemployment, a record number of bankruptcies, and closure of factories are among the concerns that have kept many governments awake.

Opportunities and Risks

To sustainability champions, the lockdowns of cities in major economies offer fresh opportunities for major policymakers to reset their economies in a sustainable manner in the post-pandemic era. Going green represents a renewed window of opportunity for many Western economies. With much less traffic on highways, thousands of planes grounded at airports, and factories remaining shut, scientists all around the world have noticed cleaner air and ecological changes in surrounding nature and parks. Nitrogen dioxide pollution in United States was recorded to be down by at least 30 per cent; elsewhere, air pollution was cut by easily 50 per cent in the major cities of Beijing, Shanghai, Paris, and New Delhi. These positives are unlikely to last when economic activities start to return to pre-pandemic levels.

In the 7 May 2020 issue of *Financial Times*, experts reminded the world of the consequential risks from the lessons learned in the pandemic. An immediate question is whether countries have in place a range of preventive measures to cope with the impacts of the climate change. Lessons from the pandemic were obvious. Preventive measures could have saved thousands of lives.

The *Financial Times* article quoted a Morgan Stanley report that in 2017, a total of sixteen weather and climate disasters in United States alone cost the government USD 309 billion. Morgan Stanley estimated global losses from climate-related disasters for the past decade at a total of USD 3 trillion. These figures have made some governments worried, while others preferred to wait and see.

Despite many visible actions and big commitments from policy and corporate leaders, greenhouse emissions are expected to rise. The BBC reported on 5 May 2020 that a total of 3 billion people could live in extreme heat by the year 2070, based on a UN population projection. The UN report pointed out that the data on warming scenarios has projected a possible 3 °C increase, doubling what was agreed upon at the Paris climate change convention in 2016.

According to this UN report, unless greenhouse gas emissions fall dramatically, 3 billion of the planet's inhabitants will be subjected to heat temperature of more than 29 °C. Heat waves in major cities are becoming common. A 50 °C temperature will become the norm, leaving cities experiencing water shortages. Dry weather is not only bad for city dwellers but also farmers. It affects the whole supply chain within the food industry.

Major economies are committed to the seventeen sustainable development goals (SDGs). Despite laudable attempts, the expected reduction in greenhouse gas emissions among the major polluters has been slow. The next ten years will determine whether there is any chance of preventing the worst impacts of climate change, which could be orders of magnitude worse than the Covid-19 pandemic disruption. If by 2030 we have not cut greenhouse gas emissions by half globally, we will not be able to avoid devastating tipping points that would shatter the global economy and pose existential human threats. The costs of inaction are staggering: $600 trillion by the end of the century.

According to the British-based Christian Aid, at least fifteen extreme weather disasters occurred in 2019 that could be blamed on climate change. Each of these events costs over a billion US dollars to the governments. The list ranges from wildfires in California and Australia to floods in the United States.

Capacity

Within this context, the United Nations is keen to ensure that member states have in place the capacity to build adaptation policies and actions. A 2019 progress update on SDGs reports that as of 20 May 2019, some twenty-eight countries had already accessed the Green Climate Fund grant to finance the formulation of national adaptation plans at a cost of USD 75 million. Many of these countries were vulnerable to rising sea levels.

The least developed countries can be given the means to access to the right technology and know-how. Some examples involve helping communities move away from low-lying areas. There are also changes in structural design in buildings to maximise heat storage or even switching crops to suit changing weather.

Cost

It is expected that during this decade, global economies will experience further climate-related disasters, not confined to the weather. The coronavirus disruption is expected to leave behind a trail of economic distortions and damages. Not surprisingly, the United Nations trade and development agency has already estimated the cost to be near to USD 1 trillion. This does not include the tragic human consequences or the disruption to world trade and uncertainty in national economies.

Many experts have already predicted that if these figures are shocking, the cost of climate change consequences would be even more staggering—USD 600 trillion, according to the *Financial Times* report. There are already signs of climate change effects that will not only be distracting but destructive. The pandemic has demonstrated the fragility of every society, and the destructive tipping points of climate change will cut off their lifelines, threatening global economies that billions depend on.

Climate change is a massive threat much bigger than the pandemic. Unpredictable weather makes it difficult for governments and businesses to provide instant solutions, unlike the health preparedness many have witnessed from the response to the spread of Covid-19. While the pandemic can inflict pain, inconvenience, and even death, climate change from forest fires to storms can affect economies, reduce food security, and threaten public health and stability.

The United Nations report further confirmed that unreasonable CO_2 levels can reduce the nutritional value of crops. Some experts refer to climate change as a slow burn. The adverse effects take years, but farmers from the United States to India have seen production fall from changes in climate over the past decades.

Recovery packages will cost trillions of dollars. As seen in pandemic responses, not all governments will have the deep resources necessary to finance infrastructural support at the scale needed to tackle global disasters. As seen in the way countries were affected by the pandemic, the potentially devastating consequences of climate change will pose challenges to the health and social systems of many developing and emerging nations.

The vulnerability of many public health systems, even in advanced nations, were exposed during the pandemic. Long periods of drought can have a direct causal effect on poverty and, in the longer term, may even spur an outflow of economic and environmental refugees, causing stress in neighbouring countries. Both the threats of poverty and possible infectious diseases are harmful to society.

Governments, having experienced the pandemic, should give the same urgency to addressing the UN's SDGs by redirecting infrastructure restoration and development. Equally important, the rescue package worth billions should be invested responsibly and sustainably. Natural resources ought to be used in a more responsible and sustainable manner in line with the principles prescribed in the SDGs. The importance of sustainability movements is without a doubt relevant in the current context, especially so in public health, where the pandemic has exposed the system's fragility.

New Investment

The pandemic crisis has encouraged governments not to lose sight of their commitment to a low-carbon agenda. Technology on decarbonation and digitalisation has made all these more possible and accessible.

Governments and the private sector can work together to begin the process of cleaning up the 'dirty sectors'—for example, transport and power systems. Decarbonising the power sector requires a reduction in carbon intensity, and this is part of the actions to be taken by countries committed to emissions reduction in the Paris Agreement. Rapid decarbonisation of the power sector is necessary as sectors such as transport start to make electric cars more mainstream. The proposal by the European Union to link its 750 billion euro economic stimulus to its climate goals, if successfully implemented, will help its member state Poland increase its renewable energy by 65 per cent, which will substantially cut down the country's reliance on coal to generate its power supply.

Investment in new energy technology to take carbon out of the atmosphere includes carbon capture and storage. Use of solar and wind energy substitution technologies will create demand for new skills in technical, engineering, and managerial talent in new energy, environmental management, and sustainability management. It is the joint efforts of public–private partnership that will create the economies to grow green industries, allowing the rise of an appropriate talent supply in the sustainability or environmental disciplines.

There are short-term challenges coming from the traditional fossil fuel industry, especially so when prices have fallen to an all-time low. But by the same token, the prices of technology for solar and wind energy have also fallen, by as much as 80 per cent. Governments must take the lead in this investment in public utilities. For this to happen, both political will and commitment would be needed, and push from regulators will not be simple as there are vested interests to consider and resistance to overcome.

The European Commission has taken the lead as part of its commitment to prepare a comprehensive recovery plan that prioritises digital and renewable energy transformation. While this may be true, the International Energy Agency (IEA) has already warned in a report in the *Times* of 27 May 2020 that global investment in green sectors may fall, with a drop in the number of installations of rooftop solar panels and wind and solar farms, with an expected 10 per cent decline in power-sector spending. The IEA also predicted that green projects will be affected by the physical restrictions on development during lockdowns of major cities.

New Skills and Know-How

One of the pandemic opportunities in advanced economies is that new clean energy projects will be the first to resolve the structural shift in job creation and help generate growth of new jobs as a result of the potential spin-off within the supply chain of green industries. There will be job opportunities in waste management, green financing, and sustainable agriculture. Governments will have the opportunity to be committed to incentivising investment in human capital while creating opportunities for sustainable career development across the greener industries.

The growth in green-collar jobs is expected to increase as the global economy eventually recovers, offering fresh hope for new jobseekers to find career opportunities and renewed hope for those out of work to be reabsorbed into the new low-carbon economy as part of structural change. Transitioning to a green economy requires concerted efforts and cooperation among the various government agencies and industries. There will need to be legislative reforms, including heath standards, and these will take time.

Fundamentally, the biggest challenge will be the need for new technology, which is exactly what China has attempted to do: identify, acquire, and innovate the right technology. Then there is the need to develop fresh talent, as this will take time to source and develop. Investment in research, education, and development will be necessary to support the new industries.

Nature

The pandemic crisis has also reminded global leaders of the importance of respecting nature and wildlife. This has been the case with previous diseases, from Ebola to severe acute respiratory syndrome (SARS) and avian and swine flu. These experiences have one thing in common: the viruses that led to the diseases all originated from animals. The World Wildlife Fund (WWF) recently produced a report, 'The Loss of Nature and Rise of Pandemics: Protecting Human and Planetary Health', that warned governments of the risks of future outbreak of pandemics that could be even more deadly if steps are not taken to crack down on illegal wildlife trade, unregulated markets, and destruction of biodiversity. Wildlife from pangolins to bats were caught in the thousands in

Malaysia and slaughtered for human consumption in China, Indonesia, and Vietnam.

The *Guardian* on 27 April 2020 reported urgent warnings from the world's top scientists for a halt to the destruction of nature lest we suffer even worse pandemics. The UK-based newspaper echoed the WWF report in affirming a close link between human damage to ecosystems and emergence of deadly infectious diseases. The WWF report regards the pandemic crisis as an urgent wake-up call for in-depth reflection on the relationship between humans and nature and the risks and consequences that often come with developmental activities. It called for a new deal to reverse loss of nature as part of the Paris climate accord.

Scientists, in the WWF report, reminded governments that various economic rescue packages must include commitments to strengthen and enforce environmental protection. The scientists have warned that 'It may be politically expedient to relax environmental standards and to prop up industries such as intensive agriculture, airlines, and fossil fuel–dependent energy sectors, but doing so without requiring urgent and fundamental change essentially subsidises the emergence of future pandemics.'

To sum up on the pandemic opportunities, *Forbes*, in its 11 April 2020 issue, identifies possible areas governments and societies should pick up from the pandemic. The first reinforces what was said in the WWF report, which is the nonseparation of human health and natural habitats. The influential magazine among the business community reinforced what experts have already said. To quote:

> Despite the many warning signs, humans have become a geophysical force as we continue to destroy, pollute and poison on a

massive scale the very foundation we depend on for survival and wellbeing. Every year we dump over 30 billion tons of carbon into the atmosphere. We destroy entire animal and plant species at an alarming rate. We have cut down forests everywhere. We poison the soil and the water, and our garbage covers the floors of the oceans. And yes, every year, we kill over 100 billion animals to feed our carnivorous appetites. Our industrial-era mind-set of 'growth at any cost' has become a recipe for self-destruction. We have long known that markets cannot succeed in failing societies. Now we must learn that healthy societies and markets depend on the health of the natural environment.

The second important opportunity is for science to be given its place to play a bigger role in public debates and policies. It must become an influential voice to protect public interest and health. *Forbes* reminded the world community that while many national governments are self-reliant, they cannot work alone to confront the global threats of the pandemic crisis. An infectious virus has no national identity; it does not stop for border checks or discriminate on basis of ethnicity, religious faith, or preferences. Yet the recent experiences of most advanced nations tend to suggest a divergence and emergence of national self-interest.

Choices

If there are opportunities offered by the pandemic for governments to go green, there are also risks that all of these may end up in academic references that many political and community leaders wish to ignore or forget. The new normal would demand a fresher look that includes discarding old habits and forcing many to better understand a more sustainable future. Choosing the right actions and seizing opportunities depends largely on how many, especially in government, are prepared to let go of practices that have harmed humanity.

The pandemic crisis is just a preliminary test. Bigger challenges in sustainability matters will come that will further test leaders who were given a longer time to prepare in both their capacity to respond and ability to make the most of opportunities.

CHAPTER 7

Compliance

In today's business context, it is not uncommon to find disciplines such as environment, health, and safety (EHS) treated as important but necessary elements of business strategies and plans. Such changes are necessary for growing business profitability and recognise that EHS is not a matter of compliance and cost. The acceptance of EHS as a strategic imperative is in line with the sustainability movement. It gives a better meaning to the concept of sustainability, which is 'meeting the needs of the present generation without impairing the ability of future generations to meet their own requirements'.

Triple-Bottom-Line Commitment

There are easily hundreds of global and local businesses in various capital markets that have in place a *triple bottom line* basis, which embraces and recognises the important synergy between profits and environment and social considerations. Most countries have at least one basic environmental law. But a 2019 United Nations report revealed that very few nations comply with their own environmental policies. The report was startling and ironic, given increasing number of environmental concerns. It is no secret that the rate of deforestation is alarming, and with it the threats to biodiversity.

Environmental laws are universal. It is necessary for international firms that do business overseas to know environmental law, where the landscape is constantly changing. More so, there is a growing trend of governments to insist that businesses comply with rising EHS standards that sometimes can be complex and more rigorous.

In today's unpredictable environment, noncompliance to any regulation, including those of EHS, can derail a company or prevent strategic objectives from being achieved. Companies are faced with many more external risks and controls, so assurance of better compliance management becomes even more relevant and crucial.

Beyond Financial

Today's businesses are no longer measured and judged by financial performance alone. More balanced performance management will include the effective implementation of sustainability compliance—for example, the adoption and implementation of environmental, social, and governance needs—as well as comply with and respect local cultural and legal requirements. The inclusion of a sustainability performance framework will ensure that areas on human rights; antibribery and corruption; human trafficking; and health and safety have universal standards.

Compliance goes hand in hand with policy where necessary to ensure that all these requirements are in line with expectations. The regulatory shift is now towards ensuring better risk management of the various sustainability-related initiatives as well as focusing on building capability around compliance culture and processes.

It is now a mainstream business practice to have in place a compliance framework that enables risk issues to be addressed before they can cause any harm. With increasing regulation, businesses and society will find it necessary to know the risks and manage them well in the context of long-term sustainability. Addressing matters on proper governance from boardroom performance to compliance to regulations will require a disciplined approach.

Supply Chain

To stay ahead of market demands and expectations, successful businesses have gone green, moving towards greater environmental and social compliance. For example, the process to ensure product sustainability is in place within the supply chain, and this is considered an important element for success. Production today embraces adoption of more sustainable substances for products and environmentally friendly or green energy design and innovative waste management.

In business, applied sustainability is essentially to ensure that a business can continue to thrive indefinitely. Some of the most successful businesses have already embraced this dedication to long-term success—for example, adhering to the principle that every resource that is being utilised needs to be replaced eventually. Businesses are recognizing that focusing on an effective framework that embraces the principles of sustainability means going beyond simple compliance.

It is expected that the standards of environmental law are likely to rise, resulting in a deliberate policy to reduce carbon footprints. Tighter regulation is expected, and indeed, in the European Union, member countries are expected to harmonise their environmental regulations and enforcement. The European Union is committed to reducing carbon emissions and introducing new directives, including an enforcement ban on harmful chemicals. It is expected that member states will follow the new regulations.

Respecting Laws

Environmental laws have moved up the agenda for most governments, as public demand continues to rise and tolerance lessens towards adverse impacts on the environment from economic developments. Large-scale forest fires, deforestation, and air and water pollution are among the many complaints, not only in advanced markets but in most parts of the earth.

Environmental laws vary around the world. There are also differing standards towards enforcement. But tolerance levels are decreasing, even in countries where local authorities are known to have received bribes for offences, including pollution of the surrounding community. In today's complex global supply chain of production, there is relevance to environmental compliance on not only products but also material for production.

In a connected world, it is even more important to pay attention to the fine details. What information is available is constantly being read, interpreted, and compared by various stakeholders. Take Volkswagen's emission scandal in 2015 for example. The global automaker agreed to a multibillion-dollar settlement with US authorities over a discovery that Volkswagen installed undisclosed software which underreported the emissions of its diesel cars sold in the United States. The US Environmental Protection Agency found the German auto giant guilty of cheating and fraud. The authorities also questioned the company's values, sincerity, and responsibility. The company not only had to pay a hefty bill but its share prices fell and its reputation was tarnished.

Public Trust

Public reaction is the most important element of success criteria. Many companies have built public trust by credibly demonstrating transparency that brings about a broader focus on ethics and its role in driving business strategy. Corporate ethics are now embedded in the implementation of company codes of professional conduct and standards that include bribery, corruption, unethical behaviour, and even wrongful expense claims.

The entire ecosystem supply chain is now being regarded as an area where priorities will be placed on environmental risk and compliance management. There is now a higher demand for standards on products, including safety and health. As such, it is not a surprise that many businesses, including those from production to delivery, are encouraging their suppliers to apply the standards in line with procurement policies. Indeed, this has become a standard requirement of all potential vendors wanting to be part of the supply chain of global businesses.

Money Laundering

An important area in which regulators have come down hard is the problem of money laundering. The International Compliance Association defines *money laundering* as the process by which criminals disguise the original ownership and control of the proceeds of criminal conduct by making such proceeds appear to have derived from a legitimate source.

The majority of nations have now put in place appropriate compliance regulations against money laundering and financing of terrorism. Aiming at banks and financial services, authorities will require a 100 per cent compliance and necessary processes, which would require establishment of compliance departments; stringent monitoring and analysis; education and guidance; and constant updates. Penalties can be extensive and include criminal charges and jail sentences.

It was in 2012 that HSBC bank was found guilty of money laundering by the US Justice Department. The bank agreed to pay a record USD 1.92 billion in fines, according to a Reuters report. The bank admitted its failure to detect that a drug cartel from Mexico was attempting to launder its money into the United States.

Given that an increasing number of businesses have built an extensive supply chain in their production activities, for them to be sustainable, they need to go beyond compliance. Hence embracing environmental and compliance stewardship is a crucial part of business strategy.

Reputation

An important element of this strategy is to ensure that corporate reputation goes beyond the first impression. A reputation for environmental responsibility is no different, as it involves trust in the brand as well as a representation of good corporate citizenship.

Business scandals relating to violation of environmental laws have not only damaged community trust but caused irreversible damage to the environment and communities.

This can lead to civil penalties. Risk-management strategies will involve compliance with environmental laws and standards, but the complexity of upholding the standards of compliance increases for global companies operating in diverse markets.

The challenge of human trafficking involving exploitation of persons often cross boundaries of country in a variety of forms from forced labour to drug trafficking continues to be widespread. The widespread abuse continues to be a challenge in both advanced and emerging nations. The focus for businesses that operate across countries is to ensure they comply to international, standards and compliances. More so in countries with less strict enforcement on such international laws and standards. Recent allegations of rubber glove companies exploiting foreign labour and human trafficking have led to refusal of certain markets to accept their products. Such complaints have dented the reputation of these companies to some extent, but it does illustrate the seriousness of markets taking such matter.

There is no doubt of the advantages of a systematic approach to social and environmental responsibility. Putting standards of compliance in place, especially cultural aspects and behaviours can lead to greater efficiency and savings. There is no dispute over the importance of reputation, which does make a difference when all products and services are otherwise equal in look, feel, and touch.

CHAPTER 8

Health

A recent World Health Organization (WHO) report warns that climate change could worsen the spread of infectious disease in the coming decades. The report highlights the fact that rising temperatures can indirectly lead to animals being carriers of disease, especially in more crowded and unhygienic environments, make pathogens better at surviving in hot climates and possibly weaken the human body's immune response.

The Covid-19 pandemic is the biggest threat to humanity in this century to date. The spread of unknown diseases, let alone an undiscovered virus, would be much more deadly than the experience with severe acute respiratory syndrome (SARS) in 2002–04, which infected 8,000 people worldwide. The Covid-19 pandemic threatens a breakdown of the public health system, on top of creating chaos in support systems across each economy and society. There is no immediate vaccine, despite early promises made by political leaders.

Global Concern

Dame Minouche Shafik, director at the London School of Economics, finds the attempt by each nation state to tackle such a global pandemic to be insufficient, as in the interconnected world, the risk of the virus returning is high. In a self-reliant world, global communities need to tackle such threats from a global front. This echoes what former UN Secretary General Kofi Annan said when he referred to the global challenges of climate change, pandemics, and terrorism as 'problems without passports' that cannot be stopped at borders, only through international cooperation. Such powerful opinions lend weight to the importance of sharing resources and cooperating at highest level.

The geopolitical challenge of two of the world's most powerful nations, China and the United States, are barriers to making this happen. Blaming each other for starting the pandemic is unhelpful. As of September 2020, more than 900,000 people have died, and the number of infections has already exceeded 30 million. The European Union has admitted that more could be done in international efforts, as this would provide a multilateral body, such as the World Health Organisation, with the resources and help it needs to respond to this extraordinary challenge.

A short history reminds global leaders and governments of the outbreak and impacts of SARS in 2002-2004. The SARS outbreak removed USD 40 billion off the world's market. While there were other infectious diseases, it is important to recognise that the majority of these emerging diseases that become so infectious come from animals.

It is well documented that contact with wild animals—from bats and monkeys to pangolins—have led to outbreaks of Ebola or SARS. Not surprisingly, studies have traced such diseases to the hunting and slaughtering of these animals for human consumption. It is recognised that such practices have always been there throughout history, especially in China, Indonesia, and many parts of Africa.

WWF Report

The recent report from World Wildlife Fund (WWF) entitled 'The Loss of Nature and the Rise of Pandemics' reaffirms the scientific theory that there is a close link between the impact of human activities on ecosystems and biodiversity and the spread of certain diseases. The report shows there are possible grave consequence of clearing forests and capturing and consuming wild animals. It is already a proven theory that any removal of habitats of wild animals creates risks to public health and safety.

The annual clearing of virgin jungles in the forests of Indonesia has gotten worse, and during the dry seasons, thousands of hectares of burned forests produce a haze that covers major cities of neighbouring Malaysia and Singapore. The report highlights, among other issues, the massive risk of outbreak of animal-borne infectious diseases, such as the Covid-19 pandemic. The transmission of diseases from animals is not new, but the Covid-19 pandemic presented the most significant threat to global economies, health, and safety.

The WWF has been campaigning against the illegal and uncontrolled trade of live wild animals for decades. Its report reinforces the risk of such bad practices, which often bring dangerous opportunities for contact between humans and the diseases these animals carry. The report rightly reiterates the common view among leading scientists that the ancient practice of trading in wild mammals, birds, and reptiles creates the right conditions for the development and spread of infectious diseases that can turn into global pandemics.

WWF reported a research by the Campus Bio-Medico University of Rome that suggests the current pandemic may have originated from bats sold live and slaughtered in Chinese markets. Today, some of these wild animals are smuggled from other countries for different purposes. One common example is Malayan pangolins, which are in demand for traditional Asian medicine as well as for their meat.

Despite international agreements classifying these transactions as illegal, thousands of animals end up in unhygienic conditions, where they are kept, slaughtered, and processed. This illegal trade is worth billions. Despite China's recent ban on eating wild animals, such unregulated wildlife, sales will likely continue, as more government enforcement and commitments would be necessary.

The vulnerability of public health was exposed in many countries during the outbreak of Covid-19. In many advanced countries, amid a breakdown in the economic system, there was no economic assistance from the government.

Campaigns

The WHO has been spending much of its resources on both awareness and capacity building, including specified attention paid to both technology and necessary infrastructural system and support. The work to eliminate infectious diseases of malaria, polio, tuberculosis, and the like never ends, and WHO has also been recognised for its leadership towards improving life expectancy and child mortality rates, especially in poorer countries.

These accomplishments are in line with the United Nations sustainable development goal of 'Ensure healthy lives and promote well-being of people of all ages'. Attaining such a goal by the year 2030 is by no means straightforward;

ensuring good health is very much dependent on other influencers, including funding, access, opportunities, and climate issues. Inclusivity in promoting well-being at all ages is essential to sustainable development. Many governments do work with multilateral agencies and are more than aware of other issues, including education, access to low-carbon technologies, and public policies.

Beyond ecology lies the danger of climate change, present and future. It is now recognised as a risk to human health. This is because as global temperatures fluctuate, with extreme heat or unpredictable rainfalls, these environmental concerns will affect air quality, water supplies, and even food security. An example of the latter can be seen in rising air or water pollution, where environmental toxins and changes in weather patterns easily affect food supplies and eventually cause health problems. Already there are fears that climate change can cause a fresh influx of environmental refugees as well drift from rural areas into urban centres.

Weather

Much media publicity has centred on the melting of the ice caps in Antarctica. These are likely to cause sea levels to rise by as much as 1.3 metres by the year 2100 if the earth's surface continues to warm by another 3 to 3.5 °C. According to a study in the journal Climate Atmospheric Science, the melting of the ice sheets covering Antarctica will cause the oceans to rise even higher. New projections for both the 2100 and 2300 horizons are significantly higher than those from the UN Intergovernmental Panel on Climate Change (IPCC), including a special report on ocean pollutions released in September.

It is also worrying that scientists and researchers are expecting the worst from the impacts of the climate change. According to their projections, the number of deaths will rise to about 250,000 per year between 2030 and 2050. The cause of death can include such climate-related conditions as heat stress, hunger, and even trauma, as extreme weather and natural disasters can be stressful for people, especially older generations. One of the tipping points has been record temperatures recorded in major cities in recent years. It is not only hot but the high temperature comes with air pollution and higher incidences of cough and related illnesses.

Another worrying piece of evidence reported in the *Independent* is the unusual heatwave in Siberia of 38 °C during the early part of June 2020. Scientists have warned that such an unusual weather gave rise to the threat of dormant viruses being revived. They further cautioned that rapid warming of the Arctic would free bacteria trapped in the ice for centuries. Similar to the Covid-19 pandemic, scientists have warned that the threat will be deadly if these viruses come into contact with humans.

Climate change has been blamed for the number of forest fires and extreme flooding that have indirectly contributed to the rise in posttraumatic stress disorder and high levels of anxiety due to the shock of having to go through such stressful experiences. According to the Centres for Disease Control and Prevention, the number of mental health–related issues is also on the rise, such as suicide, depression, and mental illness. There has even been an emergence of rodent-borne diseases associated with flooding, which would be expected to be more frequent as climate change becomes more frequent.

There is already evidence of possible climate change scenarios in which causes and effects are already well documented. Sustainability is all about using resources responsibly and ethically. Conflicts between profit motives and risks have increased in number and intensity. One can expect greater campaigns from both sides, and it is clear, for example, that the exploitation of ecology and wild animals has its price. The Covid-19 pandemic, which has disrupted hundreds of markets and taken more than 400,000 lives, has proven there are limits.

Increasing Awareness

The consumption of resources and lifestyles must change. A predicted 3 °C increase in global temperature by the turn of the century is already expected and accepted by many, although campaigns in major countries are aiming for no more than what was agreed upon at the Paris climate convention in 2016. Changing weather patterns will severely affect health in various societies around the world. Heat intensity from forest fires will rise and worsen, causing a wide range of air pollutions and haze that lead to health issues.

Countering these sustainability-related concerns will require investment in sustainable technology to decarbonise, make a massive shift from fossil fuels, focus on reforestation over deforestation, and stamp out illegal trade in wild animals. All these developments will demand more awareness and movement calling for change. As Christiana Figueres and Tom Rivett-Carnac put it in their book *The Future We Choose: Surviving the Climate Crisis*, we must increase awareness, from schools to political lobbies. Public health is one of the sustainable development goals which is crucial for stability of humanity and societies.

CHAPTER 9

Food Security

The Covid-19 pandemic has exposed the risk of what would happen in a society without adequate access to a robust food security policy and practice. Food should never be taken for granted. The pandemic has caused unprecedented disruption to economies worldwide, as trading nations closed their borders in an effort to bring the spread of infection under control.

Panic

The immediate consequences of lockdowns were long queues for essentials and empty shelves at supermarkets in cities like Sydney, Kuala Lumpur, Singapore, and Milan. There were reports of hoarding of essentials. Fights broke out among locals in their rush to stock up on consumables.

Panic buying was made worse by concerns that distribution of food supplies would be disrupted by closure of national borders. In Malaysia, when channels of distribution were halted, farmers and their distributors simply dumped their produce. Some of this was subsequently taken up by charities that took the trouble to distribute it free to the underprivileged. There were others who shifted to online delivery services to link directly with customers.

The pandemic exposed the vulnerability of food distribution, especially in countries that rely on food imports. Decades of globalisation have enabled countries to build a reliable supply chain of goods transport and distribution channels. Food has become so accessible that anyone could get anything on the table with the right means. It is unthinkable to imagine the likely scenario of a world that runs out of food supply.

Food exports have been increasing for decades. According to the Moore Stephens 2019 report, *Evolving Risks in the Global Food Supply*, food exports now account for more than USD 8 trillion of global gross domestic products. Apart from China, the top ten nations accounting for more than 80 per cent of total food exports are from the advanced nations. Main food exports from the United Kingdom are largely grain and dairy products, and even China today exports much of its food supply and grains to neighbouring countries.

Supply Chain

The supply chain management for food is complex. It is driven by an interdependency network between producers, distributors, and retailers. The complex processes reflect the interconnected world we live in today, and while technology has enabled food businesses to grow, it has also created several risks.

Before the breakout of the Covid-19 pandemic, many discussions were centred on growing climate challenges and risks to global food supplies. The United Nations Food and

Agriculture Organisation (FAO) had warned of impending price hikes across all food supplies due to climate issues and political instability. More importantly, repeated incidents of severe droughts and even floods have led to market instability, causing price hikes and even food shortages.

The bigger challenge comes from the growing appetite of a growing population, especially in emerging countries. A recent FAO report warned that growing demand has meant more of the earth's resources are exploited to the fullest. Land, water, and even energy have been utilised at unprecedented levels. The report warned that the window of opportunity to address these concerns was shutting down rapidly. It stated that easily half a billion people would reside in places that would become uninhabitable, and the main culprit was climate change, which would bring threats of prolonged droughts and even floods. The consequences of such impacts are obvious: more people undernourished and a likelihood of mass migration.

The FAO has instituted several actions to help farmers adapt to climate change through a wide series of technical measures and assistance. Reducing vulnerability by teaching famers to better plan their planting seasons is one example. Fluctuations require adjustment to habits and better management of the dependencies. All these would increase efficiency in the use of water and energy resources. The ability to forecast frequent changes to weather patterns is another possible area where farmers can plan better.

In a hungry world where the total population of the planet is reaching 8 billion, the Covid-19 pandemic has thrown a huge spanner into the growing momentum of the food supply chain. The closure of national borders has posed a challenge to the global food system. There are not many countries which can claim to be self-sufficient in food. There are possibly fewer than fifteen countries in this category, including Canada, Australia, Russia, India, Argentina, Myanmar, Thailand, and the United States.

According to *National Geographic*, by the year 2050, half the world's population will depend on food produced elsewhere due to problems of diminishing arable land and shifting rural–urban migration. *National Geographic* further reports that the food system in the global world has already leveraged systems of imports and transport infrastructure.

External Shocks and Threats

Recent closure of national borders has delivered a sudden shock to the system, with threats brought about by the negative effects of climate change. The world community is reminded of the fragile social and economic system. In many places, distribution of food can be easily disrupted. One lesson learnt for business is not to broaden the choice of places where they can procure multiple supplies.

While experience has shown possible short-term food shortages, should the disruption to the supply chain be prolonged, this may change. Prices will inevitability increase. In many places, food affordability is a challenge.

In a nutshell, the twin challenges of the pandemic and climate change are fundamental threats to humanity and society. This does drive home the point to many countries to consider policies and practices of strengthening of food sufficiency to ensure resilience in the face of both climate and pandemic disruptions.

Learning from such early lessons reminds many of the 2030 Agenda for Sustainable Development that recognises that the world is changing fast, and there is an urgent need to face new challenges that must be overcome if we are to live in a world without the disruption to food supplies. The social menace of hunger, food insecurity, and poor health bring about unhealthy consequences to the stability of any society.

The pandemic has demonstrated the importance of using technology to manage integrating all the information in its capacity to connect and enable the supply chain to manage the possible risk of disruption, as well as exposing the possible range of risks. The country's ability to enable effective food security is also dependent on climate externalities and threats.

Access

The FAO report on *The State of Food Security and Nutrition in the World 2019* recognises the effects of climate change on food access and production. Such impacts on the availability, accessibility, and stabilisation of food systems and distribution will have wide implications on the livelihoods of many who produce, distribute, or even consume. Increasingly, countries that have experienced the impacts of the pandemic have realised the risk of social instability, joblessness, and even malnourishment among their populations.

These developments will push many countries to consider how food is being produced and distributed amongst the wider stakeholders. The threats to food security and health are real. It is therefore a must that safeguarding food security and health becomes a priority. Governments, including all their stakeholders, must recognise the importance of the risk to food security not only to survive the period of distress but also to build the capacity to manage economic uncertainty and fragility, withstand challenges, and recover rapidly.

CHAPTER 10

Responsible Investment

There are similarities between the experience gained from the economic and social disruptions of the pandemic and what could possibly happen when the system that supports fragile ecology and society finally breaks down. It was very noticeable during the pandemic how economies are interlocked with society and how much social order is dependent on the well-being of economies. Such can be observed from the absence of traffic jams and a significant drop in air and noise pollution when factories are shut, airplanes are grounded, and shops are closed.

There are renewed calls for sustainable investing from the trillions-worth of stimulus packages committed to saving economies from the expected business contraction resulting from the negative effects of the Covid-19 pandemic. It was not long ago that concern over impacts of climate change was given that attention.

Broader Agenda

McKinsey & Company believes that the global community should not ignore the broader sustainability agenda of climate change and social equality. The global consulting firm is not alone in this. On 9 June 2020, the *Guardian* published a letter signed by leaders of large businesses, charities, and business trades urging the prime minister of the United Kingdom to put UN's sustainable development goals (SDGs) at the heart of the UK's Covid-19 recovery plans, echoing many who believe that governments should seize the opportunity to address glaring problems and issues of social concerns and climate change.

The noise is even louder at the World Economic Forum (WEF). Its influential members have urged global leaders to focus on investments in climate-resistant technology in the next decade. Many global consultants believe that there is no better time to invest in low-carbon technologies; because borrowing is cheap, a lower-carbon agenda cannot be ignored. WEF, in its paper 'Could Covid-19 Give Rise to a Greener Global Future?', argues that there is every reason for markets to discard fossil fuels and replace them with renewable energy technologies which are more accessible and affordable. Despite the recent drop in the price of fossil fuel, WEF concurred with the pledges taken by the European Union to go green. A shift to a sustainable pathway is timely, especially in green infrastructures, recycling business, and regenerative agriculture, amongst the few areas identified for a possible low-carbon economy.

Given the scope and magnitude of this crisis, and the long shadow of negative economic repercussions, can the world afford not to pay attention to climate change and the broader sustainability agenda at this time? McKinsey & Company is of the view that global communities cannot. Not only does climate action remain critical over the next decade, but 'investments in climate-resilient infrastructure and the transition to a lower-carbon future can drive significant near-term job creation while increasing economic and environmental resiliency'.

There is an increasing view among experts that policymakers should seize the opportunity by resetting the social system to invest in green energy instead of fossil fuels. The commitment to restart major economies in their billions should really be focusing on low-carbon energy systems.

Socially responsible investments were once considered to be less reliable, less cost-effective, and lacking infrastructure support. Years of research and development with funding resources have made accessible technology for renewable energy now possible. From the perspective of sustainability proponents, there is no reason for governments to rethink using fiscal measures to ensure that resources are focused on low-carbon utilities infrastructure, reforestation, and support for the circular economy by investment in recycling businesses.

Sustainable Investment

ESG (environmental, social, and governance) was launched in January 2004 by former UN Secretary General Kofi Annan. With the support of the International Finance Corporation and the Swiss government, and based on the principle of global compact, the world body successfully partnered with easily fifty leading institutions. The effort received good reviews and had the support of the New York Stock Exchange. Importantly, there was also the launch of the Principles for Responsible Investment (PRI). Underpinning these principles is the business case that incorporating ESG in the capital market comes with sustainable outcomes for both investors and societies.

Studies have shown that low-carbon investments can be profitable and commercially feasible. Such investments have proven to have strong returns and have also created new jobs and, equally compelling, improved the well-being and overall health of communities. The PRI initiative today has grown into USD 70 trillion worth of assets, with a membership of more than 1,600.

The transition to a more sustainable global economy, as demanded by the SDGs, offers fresh business opportunities to investors wanting more reliable but also socially acceptable returns. From the concept of socially responsible investments to today's sustainable investing, the global investment portfolio is now worth USD 70 trillion. Investopedia defines *sustainable investing* as directing investment capital to companies that seek to combat climate change and environmental destruction while promoting corporate responsibility. It is about investing in the preservation of the ecology and resources for future progress whist recognising their governance and social responsibility.

The process of factoring the environmental, social and corporate governance (ESG) criteria into investment decisions allows investors to build their fund portfolios with a goal of measuring the environmental and social impacts alongside financial returns across renewable energy application, social inclusiveness, climate change, and community development. ESG investment has grown tenfold since 2004, according to McKinsey & Company studies. The growth has been attributed to heightened social, governmental, and consumer attention on the broader impact of corporations, as well as by investors and executives who realise that a strong ESG proposition can safeguard a company's long-term success.

Business performance reflects the weight of attention rather than a feel-good factor.

A CNBC report from 14 February 2020 highlighted the potential growth and reasons why experts would be placing their money in this business:

> 'For the first time since WWII we sense a shift in which climate and the environment—not growth—will become the priority of governments and their citizens, as shortages of food, clean water and air become existential questions,' Saxo Bank Chief Economist Steen Jakobsen said in his latest quarterly outlook report. ... Jakobsen predicted that increasing climate awareness and the growing shift in policy and behaviourur, coupled with technological advancements lowering the cost of green technologies, makes green stocks increasingly attractive.

ESG Investment Opportunities

The momentum towards ESG investing is not likely to slow down. The financial growth and returns have been consistent, as in the case of its followers. This is in line with the reported outlook from the World Economic Forum in Davos, January 2020, where ESG investing continued to receive the thumbs-up from the influential participants. Indeed, sustainability concerns—including global warming, water scarcity, and housing crises—represent global risks, and these are where the investors see potential areas of investment and returns in the future.

The future of ESG will be driven by several developments. Many investors see positive developments from Germany, where the government is committed to phasing out coal-fired plants by 2038, and China, which has already taken the lead in renewable energy and is now the number-one producer of solar panels, wind turbines, and electric vehicles. In both cases, the governments have played a major role in direct investment as well as putting in place policy developments towards the growth of such green industries. The objectives are to support decarbonisation efforts and to find substitutes so that reliance on fossil fuels is reduced. This and the shifting of consumer preferences will demand changing consumption patterns and availability of proper infrastructure, government policies, and the local climate in the region of use. Indeed, promotion of renewable energy remains a key strategy for decarbonizing the various sectors, especially power generation, transport, and industry.

Growing Demand

The increase in market growth and trends comes from the expected growth in population size to 10 billion by the year 2050. The global demand for resources, energy, and food will mean a call for additional infrastructure that must be accessible and easily fundable.

The United Nations *Global Sustainable Development Report 2020*, however, recognises that external funding is necessary to support improvements that will allow countries to build better resilience against future humanitarian crises as experienced in the battle against the global Covid-19 pandemic. Not only does the report showcase the need for greater partnership towards SDGs, the global community is to be reminded of the opportunities in areas such as health, energy, and biodiversity.

The report highlights opportunities that have allowed millions access to newer sources of energy but also accepts that the use of renewable energy is the key to the realization of human and social well-being for the future. The multilateral body knows that to reduce the global carbon footprint, renewable energy must gain a bigger share of energy consumption. The expansion of solar photovoltaics and wind is healthy, but transport and household sectors' continuous reliance on fossil fuel will not help with SDGs.

Rapid technological advances in computer sciences, artificial intelligence, and biotechnologies hold the promise of providing solutions to many of the challenges facing SDGs, including those that involve difficult trade-offs. For example, technology can facilitate accessibility to build transport and information facilities. Improving connectivity can help promote social inclusion to realise the full and equal participation of all in society, including the 1 billion persons with disabilities worldwide.

At the same time, technological innovations risk further entrenching existing inequalities, introducing new ones, and, through unintended consequences, setting back progress towards the 2030 agenda. For example, without access to digital infrastructure and accessible information and communication technology, persons with disabilities are at increased risk of being excluded from statistics and surveys used to develop future programmes and policies.

Future industries associated with clean water and food are at the top of every government's priorities. It is equally important to mass transport for capital funds to be made a priority, especially in overcrowded and traffic-congested cities. The mass transport rail and electric vehicles are the shape of sustainability that will characterise future cities.

There is no shortage of ideas and opportunities, but investing sustainably and responsibly is the right move to ensure sustainability momentum. Better coordination between government and business is necessary, and such partnerships can be profitable if the investment is effectively deployed for ESG purposes to serve the greater good.

CHAPTER 11

Electric Vehicles

Electric vehicles are not new. These innovations were introduced to the market more than a century ago. Past decades saw a rise in popularity for electric cars for a variety of reasons. It was first attributed to lower cost of maintenance, especially during the era of high energy costs. Electric vehicles have also made significant improvements in performance, design, and maintenance. Electric cars are far more efficient, through their capacity to convert 80 per cent of energy from battery into performance.

Growth and Controversy

According to the Global Electric Outlook 2020, the sales of electric cars have reached 2.1 million globally. The *Markets Insider*, however reported that the electric vehicle market was worth USD 39.8 billion in 2018 and will be at nearly USD 1.5 trillion by the year 2025. Electric vehicles are the future and part of the vision of how the earth should embrace global goals on reduction of the carbon footprint. Electric vehicles are regarded as a convenient reason and an important mitigating step to overcome the challenge of limiting carbon emission to no more than 2 °C, as agreed at the Paris climate outcomes in 2016. Carbon Brief reinforced this argument based on analysis in a report on climate impacts of electric vehicles. According to the report, electric vehicles do generate considerably less carbon emissions than, say, average conventional cars.

There are others who would argue that while it is true that electric vehicles generate less carbon, there are emissions from production of parts used to manufacture electric vehicles. There are even critics of electric vehicles who would make claims that electric cars will make no significant impact on carbon emissions. One example is a working paper from a group of German researchers from the Institute for Economic Research who claimed that in the best scenario, the carbon emission produced from battery-driven cars would be higher than that of a diesel engine.

To many governments, the amount of emissions is measured through output from fuel cycle and use of materials rather than the production of the vehicles. It is known that electricity generation and utilisation would be far less than conventional vehicles. Using electric vehicles powered by lower-carbon electricity makes sense, although the battery can be expensive and recharging may not be as convenient as conventional vehicles. In the United Kingdom alone, emissions from electricity generation dropped by close to 40 per cent and well within the target of more than 70 per cent by the year 2030.

There are further examples of research undertaken to justify the returns in terms of emission numbers. Another example is the IVL Swedish Environmental Research Institute's analysis of recent battery-driven cars such as the Tesla Model 3 and Nissan Leaf.

Investment Trends

The past decade has seen the major car producers investing in research and development for electric cars. A BDO report in 2019 shows that the top twenty carmakers in the world spend more than a USD 100 billion a year on research and development in electric vehicles. The accounting and advisory firm reports that this is part of the transition plan of automakers towards electric and autonomous vehicles. The move is largely driven by the government's commitment to a lower carbon footprint. Such regulatory pressure is also part of a long-term plan to end petrol- and diesel-fuelled vehicles. The aggressive drive is more of a move towards ultralow emission by the year 2030, according to the report.

Much of the push is driven by regulators who have a commitment to make the auto industry go green. For example, the European Union countries are committed to a series of climate change interventions. Germany, in 2016, announced it would phase out internal combustion engines by the year 2030. This is not surprising, for Germany has been one of the advanced countries to push for low-carbon economy.

But Germany is not alone. Others, like Norway, Sweden, and Japan, have official targets for electric car preferences. Not only has there been an increase in public funding in the form of more state fiscal measures—including trade tariffs, subsidies, and incentives to invest in new technologies—there has been a consistent push towards better awareness of clean technology for transport of the future.

The economic realities include scaling up growth with the global supply chain of users and producers to encourage greener lifestyles and environment. The European Union has started legislating on limits of carbon emissions allowable. To prevent backlash from industry and consumers over a lower gasoline price, the respective governments would need to give more fiscal incentives, including removal of subsides to fossil fuels. In the era of low oil prices, the carbon pricing will be costly. The only consolation is that these market prices will fluctuate.

Electric vehicles were not hot items during a booming economy in the late 1990s. With gas prices low, consumers were not too concerned over fuel efficiency. But that did not deter Chinese companies from investing in electric vehicles. Geely and BYD were the first to experiment with electric vehicles in one of the most promising markets for the auto industry in the past two decades.

Tesla

A recent Bloomberg report puts Tesla on course to become the world's most valuable carmaker. Tesla has invested major resources in electric cars, and it tops the list of carmakers devoting lots of money in research and development of electric vehicle technology. According to a BDO report, Tesla has also invested billions in battery-driven cars in its factory in China.

Globally, according to BDO, European auto manufacturers spent the most on R & D, recording a total of GBP 33.3 billion in 2018 and 2019—35 per cent more than the GBP 24.6 billion spent in 2014 and 2015. The report further mentions that Chinese carmakers increased their R & D expenditure by 80 per cent to GBP 2.7 billion in 2018, despite starting at a low base of GBP 1.5 billion in 2014-2015. BDO is of the opinion that European carmakers are very much motivated by government incentives offered to purchasers.

In Norway alone, Tesla has a 25 per cent market share. The company is showing the world that electric cars can be as good if not better than any of the better-known cars that run on gas or diesel. It also uses sustainable energy and does not compromise on performance, looks, and price.

Research and Development

The German carmaker BMW, not to be left behind, has raised its R & D budget to USD 8.6 billion to deliver twenty-five battery-driven models by the year 2025. A number of new models between the period of 2020–2030 are expected to run on electricity. Volkswagen, BMW, and even Ford are all expected to roll out many more E versions of new models. The revival of interest in electric vehicles started more than two decades ago. A hybrid version, the Toyota Prius, was one of the first electric vehicles to appear on the road.

The push towards electric cars came when Tesla started to raise eyebrows among global carmakers with its products and consumer interest. Today, the debate over consumer choice has gone beyond price into convenience and reliability. Higher life-cycle batteries make a lot of difference. This includes even the energy being used to manufacture the battery and all the body parts of the vehicle.

Interestingly, Tesla produces batteries in plants driven by renewable energy. This suggests that the likely emission is lower than many of its competitors'. Tesla's success has pushed many of its competitors to put more effort in the direction of zero carbon footprint in this segment of the business. Over the next few years, other automakers have plans to roll out electric vehicles all around the world.

There was a time when automakers' investment decisions hinged on the global price of oil and gas. Both General Motors and Ford were victims of surging oil prices in the nineties, which led to increased preference for fuel-efficient cars offered largely by Toyota and Honda. The market share for the former was halved as a result.

Future

The period of low oil prices has recently returned, as the price has dipped below USD 30 per barrel. This translates to a much cheaper price for gasoline. Questions are being raised again on the future of electric vehicles. But they have not deterred the car industry from researching and developing fuel-efficient vehicles. Carmakers have now shifted gears towards the advancement of technology in electric vehicles.

The value proposition of electric vehicles is no longer price alone. While it is tempting for many carmakers to return to gas-guzzling vehicles, it is no longer viable, as many leading carmakers from the European Union and even China are committed to a green deal that aims to make member states carbon neutral. More so, the future will see improvements to the longer life of the battery, and the number will certainly go up.

Even then, there are challenges of trust among consumers so accustomed to petrol-driven cars to switch to electric vehicles; the necessary infrastructure support such as charging stations; and the reliability over long-distance travel. Car manufacturers nonetheless are expected to overcome these challenges, as they gear up with their improved models, as part of their commitment.

Given the awareness of carbon risks and the possible economic and social consequences if nothing is done to curb rising carbon emissions blamed for rising global temperature, the global shift towards low-carbon energy for the future is inevitable. The challenge eventually will still be at what cost to rescue our climate from becoming hotter, which brings bigger ecological and societal challenges. The answer is for all the relevant stakeholders to ensure innovation remains at the forefront to drive the change. Innovation and investment in electric vehicles are part of the zero-carbon agenda. Although carmakers may either be incentivised by government assistance or purely economic decisions to transit to electric vehicles, it remains a proposition of a low-carbon direction that can positively contribute to the global battle to halt the expanding carbon footprint.

CHAPTER 12

Going Robotic

When the BBC reported that 20 million manufacturing jobs could be replaced by robots by 2030, it caused many to fear whether such prospects would be socially acceptable. According to the *Harvard Business Review*, almost half all jobs in the US economy could be made obsolete. Yet the fear that automation in the form of robots with enhanced artificial intelligence (AI) capabilities will destroy jobs is not entirely true.

There are reports that while it is true that some jobs have been replaced by automation, such cases tend to be in the lower-skilled category, or the nature of such work involves unpleasant work conditions and so these jobs attract little interest among jobseekers. An example is the waste management business, where the use of robotic arms to sort and organise recycled materials has been one of the recent innovations.

Science Advancement

Rapid advancement in science and innovation has led to a widespread explosion of inventions and improvements within the fourth industrial revolution. These developments have made a great deal of difference and added conveniences to the movement and connectivity of people globally. Robotics have equally made many positive impacts. It is already a big business carrying great prospects for a better lifestyle—safer, cleaner, and healthier. According to Robotics Online, 'the market for professional services robotics is expected to reach a value of $37 billion between 2019 and 2021, according to the International Federation of Robotics (IFR). Between 2019 and 2021, it is predicted that the market will grow an average of 21% each a year.'

Japan leads the world in the field of robotics, especially with its investment in research and development and deployment of robotics across industries and services. The University of Tokyo reported that today, Japan employs over a quarter of a million industrial robot workers. In the next fifteen years, it is estimated that number will jump to over 1 million. Robotics revenue by 2025 is expected to reach $70 billion.

The social impact of robots may not be obvious to many. Automation, from the days of the first industrial revolution, has always been controversial. But as seen in all industries, from agricultural to mining, the substitution for human labour when there are dangers of chemical exposure has proven to be a plus not just for better health and safety but higher productivity.

Contributions

The robotics revolution started way back in the 1930s in the manufacturing sector. Innovations have evolved since then, covering a wider selection of industry including hospitality and services and even homes, hospitals, and care homes for the elderly and handicapped. Especially in Japan, where a labour shortage is prevalent, robotic automation is ideal and makes practical sense, meeting both social sustainability and business objectives.

Finding ways through robots to improve delivery processes has been at the top of the minds of leading industrialists. It has become very evident that the use of robotics is possible in sustainable development initiatives. As a result, there are already plans for robots to a play a role in the war against climate change, as well in a circular economy, with recycling processes and use of renewable and waste materials for industry.

Robotic innovation for sustainable development is an interesting proposition, where further investment in research and innovations for both industry and education have proven their business case and benefits. Drawing from the movie character *WALL-E*, there is now a possibility that the use of robots is possible in sustainability initiatives. Already there are firms starting to leverage artificial intelligence to plan the next battle against climate change.

AI-Powered

Peter Diamandis and Steven Kotler echoed this observation in their book *The Future Is Faster Than You Think*. In their chapter on 'Exponential Technologies', they stressed that robots are entering nearly every aspect of our lives. They continued by saying today's versions are

AI-empowered, allowing them to learn on their own, operate solo and in pairs, walk on two legs, balance on two wheels, drive, swim, fly, and so on. The differences robots have made include not only the economic efficiency observed at Amazon, Tesla, GM, and retailers such as Domino's Pizza and 7-Eleven but in the areas of disaster relief and delivery of medical supplies.

Today, we are likely to see more physical robots being used to track waste levels in the ocean as well as test environmental impacts and work alongside others on forest fires, droughts, and increased sea levels, all of which are possible consequences of climate change. These would not have been possible under normal circumstances.

There is also a general acceptance that global warming has already passed the tipping point. The seventeen United Nations sustainable development goals have given clarity around pressing global concerns and a set of broad directions. The world is already racing against time, and the climate issue is one in which many have said that if global leaders and communities do not act quickly, the global temperature will exceed the agreed-upon ceiling rise of 1.5 °C.

Advanced technologies with robotics and inbuilt artificial intelligence can assist with data analytics to deal with the effects of climate change. Green robots are designed to physically battle and put out wildfires which have grown in frequency and intensity, especially in dry summers of California. Robots can detect and put out fires much more efficiently than firemen.

Helping with Waste

According to *Waste Management World*:

> Intelligent robotic systems can process almost any given waste stream and sorting capabilities can be redefined for every new market situation—even on a daily basis. Furthermore, increased flexibility in recognition gives plant operators the possibility to explore new use cases.

Robotic intelligence has the capacity to scan, analyse, select, and pick up material of the same composition. It is not uncommon for robots to dismantle expired goods in such manner, hence fulfilling the recycling process and contributing to conserving resources. In such a process, robots can help humans avoid exposure to high-risk chemicals. The automation of the process improves efficiency to save energy and speed up the process of recycling.

It is a well-known fact that robots are now being deployed in the production of technologies for renewable energy. Automation of such processes not only allows better precision and speed; the whole development allows for cost savings. Many manufacturers deploy robots in desert maintenance of solar panels so that production of solar energy is optimised. Similarly, robots are deployed in large-scale farms to do the tasks of planting and ensuring an adequate amount of watering.

In waste management, robots are used to clean up pollution and ensure the cleanliness of rivers. Their tasks are to maintain the water system and prevent blockage of solid waste and plastic. Robots are designed with the flexibility to undertake any tasks, especially in areas humans may not be able to reach. Plastic waste, for example, can be found at riverbeds or even oceans, where depths are beyond the reach of humans. Their deployment is possible in all seasons, and they can only gain more prominence and use in the years to come.

With AI-enhanced capabilities, robots potentially can replace thousands of jobs at call centres, check-out counters, restaurants, as well as manufacturing and even fieldwork in rough oceans. Today, their reliability and efficiency have improved significantly, and as proven in several cases, robots are serving their purpose. It is expected that the number of robots being deployed worldwide will increase over time, as economies of both accessibility and development are reduced. Industrial robots for example, are expected to experience a rise in popularity and deployment.

In sustainability, it is recognised that robots have proven to have reduced energy consumption and have helped to improve the way waste is being disposed and managed. These have contributed towards a good cause.

Limitations

Although there are enough business and practical cases regarding the use of AI-enabled robotics technology, there are limitations as to how far the technology can be deployed. Recent surveys by PricewaterhouseCoopers and Boston Consulting Group show the number of firms planning to deploy robotic technology in their businesses has declined significantly. While the cost of deployment is an obvious factor, the use of algorithms is limited up to a certain level. It is said that robot intelligence is not equivalent to biological intelligence. Not many are convinced that the latter is replaceable in the foreseeable future. There are sceptics who believe artificial intelligence has not reached the capacity that it is expected to acquire in order to deliver.

There is no denying that AI-enabled robots do make a difference, but there is much to be done and achieved. There are already now proven cases of robots doing jobs that are presumably dangerous and harmful, and this is a way forward. But replacing human knowledge and intelligence with algorithms will take time, and there are always risks of consequences or actions that could backfire. Sustainability development demands greater input from the sciences. In the meantime, contributions from robots and AI-enabled technology have already made tangible inputs in areas that matter.

CHAPTER 13

The Plastic Menace

The UN Environment Programme (UNEP) reported in 2018 that more than 300 million tonnes of plastics are produced every year, and a high percentage of these are not recycled. This will not come as a shock to many. Millions who follow the National Geographic documentary will not be surprised to know that colossal amounts of plastic waste—about 8 million tonnes—end up in oceans. The world's leading scientists and concerned environmentalists have campaigned for years through the media and at every possible opportunity, highlighting the adverse impact of plastic waste on our ocean's wildlife as well in landfills, yet not one global leader from either government or a multinational company has been able to come up with a permanent solution.

A search of YouTube on the subject of plastic waste will find hundreds of videos proving the extent of plastic pollution, from Bali beaches to the bottom of the Indian Ocean. It is equally disturbing to read reports on bits of polystyrene found in the guts of tiny organisms in the Antarctic. The world came to know of the shocking truth of plastic waste when the media started to report on thousands of tonnes of plastic waste from advanced countries that ended their journey at ports in South East Asia.

Such bad moves became more apparent when China imposed a ban on foreign waste import, exposing the bad practice of developed markets—including the United Kingdom, Japan, Germany, and the United States—in disposal of plastic waste. Greenpeace criticised such behaviours. Its campaign director said, 'Instead of taking responsibility for their own waste, US companies are exploiting developing countries that lack the regulation to protect themselves.'

Rise of Plastic

According to the Science History Institute, the popularity of plastic surged during the 1950s, especially in the United States. Plastic substitution became an industry trend because the material was found to be durable, competitive, and versatile. Plastic gained more acceptance as it started to replace paper in packaging, steel in motor vehicles, and even wood in interior furnishings. The versatility of plastic meant such material could match or be better than its close competitors, not only in durability but also in design and shape. Plastic is also light and has an advantage over steel in motor vehicles.

For decades, plastic products have given businesses new opportunities and higher profits, and consumers the convenience and many choices. Over the years, plastic, through research and development, has become so heat-resistant that aircraft use lightweight carbon fibre that has reinforced plastics. There are now more plastic materials in motor cars than ever before. Plastic has even replaced door frames and furniture in homes.

Plastic has made its way to homes, where it becomes very much part of the disposable society where almost everything gets thrown away after a single use. From dental floss to diapers, plastic has transformed the lifestyle of households, making it convenient, easy, and even safer. For decades, consumers have used up billions of tonnes of plastic, from shopping bags to shampoo bottles. All of these have given fast-moving consumer companies—such as Unilever, Nestle, Proctor & Gamble, and Coca-Cola—the convenience of packaging and delivery of their products to established and new markets for more than fifty years.

Consequences

The documentary film *The Story of Plastic* reveals the bad consequences of plastic conveniences and the harm done to the environment and society through its waste. It reveals mountains of plastic trash that lands up in developing countries and in rivers and oceans. *The Story of Plastic* traces back the history of consumerism driven largely by multinational companies and consumer products, but even more so, the blame is on petrochemical companies that are eager and more than happy to meet the ever-growing demand for plastic.

Coca-Cola alone produces 3 million tonnes of plastic packages each year, according BBC News. That translates into 200,000 bottles per minute. One current trend, according to the *Economist*, suggests that by 2050, the amount of plastic would be more than the total fish population in the ocean by weight. Such a prediction shocked respondents in a survey in Europe to the degree that more than half would give up plastic bags forever.

Despite plastic's contributions to industry growth, consumer convenience, and ease, campaigns against its use have not died down. The momentum is largely driven by concerned civil societies and individuals who have revealed to the world the health risks to humans and harm done to the environment, nature, and wildlife. Researchers have calculated that more than 8 million tonnes of plastic waste end up in the oceans every year.

The problem of plastic waste is not going to go away easily. As the earth's human population rises, it is expected that the consumption rate of plastic will increase. So will the production of waste, from plastic bottles to household products. One immediate problem, according to scientists, is that plastic is man-made. Plastic is not biodegradable, as it contains a variety of chemicals that are toxic to everything on the planet.

Today, plastic waste is found everywhere, including places least expected—like Mount Everest, where tonnes of plastic bottles are left behind by climbers. The same observation can be made along the beaches and seas. Plastic debris is commonly found in drains in most major cities. Plastic waste poses dangers to the environment if the waste ends up clogging those drains, causing flash floods, especially in less-developed countries. According to Greenpeace, plastic trash has been found in the stomachs of seagulls, sea turtles, and even whales. Plastic waste, often in the form of plastic bottles, tubes, or bags, is mistaken for food, thus ending up in the stomachs of these marine animals and fish.

Plastic pollution poses a present and future danger not just to the ocean; uncontrolled and unmanaged plastic waste also poses health risks in cities, beaches, and forests. One of these health concerns is the discovery of microbeads from plastic waste. Will McCallum, author of *How to Give Up Plastic*, refers to *microbeads* as tiny fragments of plastic, measuring under five millimetres in diameter, found in household products. These often end up in drains and finally oceans. Such plastics are found in seafood and can cause major diseases.

Campaigns to ban plastics have so far produced actions among local governments in many markets to end single-use plastics, from drinking straws to carrier bags. An outright ban on the use of plastics requires much more effort, and includes convincing and changing human preference and lifestyle.

Educating Consumers

There are other challenges. Despite publicity campaigns and recycling efforts, educating people to reduce and reuse plastics has not significantly reduced plastic consumption. It has taken less than a century for plastic to gain as a preferred source of material by industry. It will not be an easy task to undo such advancement unless the substitutes bring equally acceptable value propositions in price and convenience.

Changing people's attitudes will require either using the economics principle by making consumers pay a higher price or an increased public campaign and education. However, there is a common belief that the fault lies with customers. Producers and big users of plastic materials for packaging do not see plastic waste as their responsibility.

One example is Coca-Cola, which publicly said it would not be phasing out the use of plastic bottle for its drinks anytime soon. At the 2020 World Economic Forum in Davos, BBC News reported that the company's head of sustainability, Bea Perez, said the reason was because

> customers value the bottles because they are lightweight and easily reseal, and argued

that getting rid of them would hurt sales. The company however intend to recycle and to use 50 percent recycled materials in packaging by that date and to work with non-profits to better collect its waste.

Recycle and Reuse

Because plastic bottles are not necessarily recyclable, critics have advocated for the use of an alternative to plastic. But not all plastic-based products are replaceable or can be recycled so easily. For example, almost every single medical supply and disposable is packed in plastic for hygiene purposes. Imagine a supermarket without plastic packaging in the fresh food section. Such plastic wrappers are not recyclable.

Some industries have acted to replace plastic containers with biodegradable packaging, while others have no plans unless there is a business case to do so. The top three sectors that use plastic are packaging, construction, and consumer. Plastic used for packaging is mostly single-use and not recyclable. This tops global users' usage and makes up half of the global production of plastic. According to Our World in Data, the lifespan of plastic for packaging is about six months, compared to thirty-five years in building and construction. This explains why packaging tops the list of sectors responsible for generating plastic waste.

Advancement in technology means there are incinerators that can burn and convert plastic waste to generate electricity. The waste-to-energy concept is gaining traction. According to *National Geographic*, the European Union is leading this field, with almost 42 per cent of its plastic waste recycled through such means. China, too, has more than three hundred waste-to-energy plants in place. But scientists have warned that when plastic is burned, it emits dangerous gas, including sulphur dioxide, hydrochloric acid, and other metal into the air, which equally pose a health risk to humans. There are experts who prefer to reduce rather than dispose, as the latter brings all sorts of unhealthy consequences.

There have been several global actions taken improve the management of plastic waste. Many local governments have taken the necessary steps to educate consumers and improve on waste disposal accordingly. There are serious attempts to consider recycling, despite the low percentage of plastic that is recyclable. While controlling and managing plastic waste are priorities, the transition to a circular economy is consider an option. Plastic will continue to be produced and perhaps even be made both in quality and quantity. Given the low price of petroleum, there is no compelling reason to push the recycling agenda unless it serves the sustainable development agenda.

Plastic Takeaways

The outbreak of the Covid-19 pandemic that led to many cities to experience lockdowns, along with the closure of boundaries, saw an upsurge in the demand for packaged food and drinks. The Sunday *Times* on 24 May 2020 covered a story on the problem of throwaway coffee cups that had been thought to be a thing of the past. Fear of the spread of the pandemic has led to high street chains halting the acceptance of reusable cups. Environmentalists, appalled by such action, have asked for reversal of the decision. The *Times* estimates that 2.5 billion disposable coffee cups are used annually, and most end up in landfills.

The spike in online delivery services during the pandemic lockdown meant more single-use plastic packaging. When authorities in Thailand ordered the closure of schools, businesses, and factories in April 2020 in an effort to curb the spread of Covid-19, the volume of plastic waste went up by 62 per cent. According to a Reuters report, this came shortly after the country banned single-use plastic bags.

Thailand is one of the world's top five plastic polluters of the ocean. It was reported that as much as 3,432 tonnes of plastic was thrown away in Bangkok daily in the month of April 2020, including plastic takeaway cutlery and bags. Concerned environmentalists feared the progress made in the campaign against single-use plastic has gone back to square one. It is also worrying for environmentalists because Thailand remains one of the top five countries contributing to ocean plastics pollution.

Equally disturbing is the headline from the *Guardian* on 8 June 2020 that reads:–'A glut of discarded single-use masks and gloves is washing up on shorelines and littering the seabed'. The newspaper reported large amounts of disposable masks floating off the Mediterranean coast. Environmentalists have also found used latex gloves at the bottom of the seabed. Experts now warn of a potential time bomb as millions of such 'Covid-waste' items could potentially be washed into the seas if not disposed of appropriately. Experts have said that face masks do contain plastics, such as polypropylene.

Partnership and Engagements

One of the proposed solutions to managing plastic waste is through international cooperation. International partnerships bring together different stakeholders to share resources and work together towards the common goal of elimination of plastic waste and microplastics.

In January 2019, the Alliance to End Plastic Waste was formed as a not-for-profit organisation to fund projects and activities aimed at addressing concerns over plastic waste. The members of the alliance are largely multinationals, including manufacturers of petrochemicals and fast-moving consumer goods. Together, they assemble resources to reuse, recycle, and recover plastic waste. Importantly, the alliance of companies is not about advocating a stop to production of plastic or considering substitutions for what they produce. The alliance's commercial interests are at stake, and this attempt is seen as adding value to help manage better the challenges within their own value chain.

The Plastic Waste Partnership established under the Basel Convention is another example where members get together to share resources for sustainability efforts. It involves diverse stakeholders from governments, academia, and civil society. There are others, including New Plastics Economy Global Commitment led by Ellen MacArthur Foundation, that work together with UNEP on recycling matters and waste management. Not all countries have the necessary commitment—let alone infrastructure, resources, and institutions—to manage plastic waste in a transparent and sustainable manner.

The scale of the problem demands resources, especially in less-developed countries. Transfer of technical know-how through science and research has helped many to push for better, more eco-friendly products and substitutions, as well promoting responsible consumerism. Government policies and leadership can make the difference. One way is to work with the private sector in a public–private sector partnership to prevent and reduce plastic waste. Elimination of plastic waste is impossible, but slowing down the process *is* possible and is part of the sustainable development obligations among governments.

A Manageable Menace

Plastic can become a menace once it turns into waste. Plastic does not decompose easily. There are enough visuals on YouTube to reinforce the message that plastic waste, if left on its own, can cause harm to the surrounding environment and even be a danger to health, safety, and society. There is no shortage of immediate solutions, from outright bans on the use of plastic to substitution. The single-use nature of plastic has been halted in the case of drinking straws or carrier bags. But plastic continues to serve its useful purpose in medical fields and, in many cases, packaging because of its versatility and flexibility.

Part of the problem is that the scale and reach of biodegradable products cannot compete against the cheaper option of plastic. There is no shortage of alternatives or innovations. There will come a time when there will be no more prepacking of consumables; food and drinks will be served on a do-it-yourself basis using biodegradable material.

Science and innovation will be necessary to expand the use of biodegradable products to be more accessible and affordable. But they must be supported and nurtured to compete against the more efficient petroleum-backed primary plastic producers. Indeed, plastic producers backed by large petrochemical companies are urging and lobbying lawmakers to reverse the ban on single-use plastic. That has kept environmentalists very alarmed and awake.

Reducing the plastic-waste footprint must be our priority if the world is serious about the menace of plastic. There is also an opportunity to change consumer behaviours, which will require not only better awareness but also their actions, including overcoming the addiction to plastic. The war is not over until plastic waste is reduced as demand for alternatives continues to rise.

CHAPTER 14

Maldives Challenges

Zubair Hassan

The Maldives is an island state located in the Indian Ocean. Officially known as the Republic of Maldives, the island state is comprised of 1,192 islands. The population of the Maldives was 515,696 at the end of 2018. The majority of the people, 142,909, resided in the capital city at the end of 2017. The Maldives enjoys a per capita gross domestic product (GDP) of USD 15,562, the highest in South Asia, up from USD 275 in 1980. The economy depends largely on tourism.

Due to the nature of their dispersed geography, the islands are vulnerable to sustainability challenges, including rising sea level due to climate change. The highest point in the Maldives is around eight feet above sea level. The average height of the coral reef islands in the Maldives is five feet above the sea level.

The Maldives faces various sustainability issues and challenges in terms of both non-climate and climate changes. The non-climate challenges—including land-use pressure and coastal erosion, waste management, limited supply of freshwater, and loss of biodiversity—could introduce challenges for the whole country, particularly the tourism sector. Rising temperature from climate change has led to coral bleaching events that make the natural resorts less attractive. This potentially impacts on tourism revenue. Since 28 per cent of the GDP comes from tourism revenue, it is important to protect the country's natural assets from excessive exploitation by human activities.

Sustainable Development Challenges

The Maldives has many unique sustainability challenges in its economics and development. Despite all these challenges, successive governments of the Maldives have been able to make significant progress in tackling the sustainable development goals of reducing poverty and hunger, increasing the number of people who can access primary education, reducing child mortality, improving maternal health, and curbing HIV/AIDS and other diseases.

The government of the Maldives recognises the threat of rising sea levels and the impact of climate change. The vulnerability of the Maldives to climate change presents a serious challenge to achieving the sustainable development goals of the country. Rising sea level, occasional flooding, and beach erosion resulting from climate change are challenges to be addressed.

As the Maldives' economy is heavily dependent on tourism, it is understandably clear that the natural environment, such as beaches, underwater marine life, coral, and many natural species, are key priorities to be protected. To support such priorities and to ensure that climate-related challenges are being addressed, a few government-led policy frameworks and projects have been initiated. One of these involves having in place a policy to review, monitor, and identify long-term sustainable development solutions.

This framework uses sustainable development goals in Vision 2020 activities and the Seventh National Development Plan. To address vulnerability gaps and barriers to implementing such policies, the government has introduced both adaptation and infrastructure development policies. The development of renewable energy sources, water resources management, and a sewerage system for each island are a few of the projects undertaken by the government.

Water Management and Sanitation

Climate change pose challenges to the freshwater accessibility and security of the Maldives. An increase in population has brought with it, urbanization and environmental change. One of the significant challenges is management of water resources and provision of sanitation services. Over the years, the demand for water in Malé has increased tremendously due to the high rate of urbanisation in Malé and some of the other islands.

Increased urbanisation pressures have led to demand outstripping supply. Integrated Water Resource Management was established to build the necessary infrastructure, including a desalination system to capture, process, and distribute clean water even during the dry season. The government is aware of the water scarcity problem due to climate change, which comes with the risk of waterborne diseases. The goal is to ensure access to a safe water supply and adequate sewerage services for 75 per cent of the population.

Access to clean water during the dry season, remains one of the priorities. Equally important is ensuring the transportation of water during the dry season.

Energy

The Maldives, like many countries, has a fossil fuel-based economy. It is highly vulnerable to price hikes that easily impact the country's balance of payment. Due to its geography, there is a challenge of storing large quantities of fuel in these islands. The current fuel-storage capacity of the country is only ten days. The practice of having to transport imported fuel into the islands two to three times a month poses risks and vulnerabilities.

To overcome this challenge, government introduced a renewable energy program in 2014 diversifying the energy sector and promoting locally available renewable energy sources. The plan is to ensure a renewable energy system that can generate up to 30 per cent of daytime in all inhabited islands at the end of 2018. In many islands, Solar PV-diesel-hybrid systems have been installed. Also, in 2016, met mast was installed in different location to assess whether wind can be used as a potential renewable energy source.

The long-term plan is to transform the energy sector so that it can produce renewable energy installation from 2MW to 21MW. Also, the government has started promoting renewable energy use at the private sector and household level. A Green Loan program was launched in collaboration with Bank of Maldives, allowing loans for those who wish to purchase renewable energy or start such projects. The government has started many initiatives, such as an awareness program for saving electricity and how to save energy among the citizens in Malé and other parts of the country.

Impacts

One of the most vulnerable countries to climate change is the Maldives. Extreme weather conditions have a significant effect on sea level, resulting in beach erosion and harm to biodiversity in low-lying coastal marine ecosystems. Also, when climate change causes the sea level to rise, resulting seawater intrusion can affect freshwater lenses on the island, which affects water security in the country.

During the tsunami of 2005, when the islands were washed by the waves, many islanders reported that their fresh water turned to salt water. There are many measures that the Maldives has taken to address climate change through adaptation and mitigation. In 2015, the government formulated a climate change policy framework to address the major concerns of climate change impact on tourism, agriculture, and other industries.

The Green Climate Fund was initiated in 2017 to support vulnerable communities and manage induced water storage during the dry season. The project was to ensure that vulnerable households have access to clean water in a cost-effective way during the dry season as part of sustainable development.

Ecosystems and Biodiversity

The Maldives is famous and popular among overseas tourists and travellers for its extraordinarily rich and diverse aquatic life. The main threats to such biodiversity in the Maldives are the loss of habitats for migrant birds, fish, and other sea species due to the overdevelopment and exploitation of human activities and climate change.

The Maldives' government has already enacted the Environmental Protection and Preservation Act (Law no.

4/93), which provides legal protection against any violation of the environment in the Maldives. This came with the National Biodiversity Strategy and Action Plan (2016–2025) to protect and address mainstream biodiversity concerns into national development planning. To overcome the risks and the vulnerability of the environment, the Maldives has designated forty-two protected areas. This allows the government to conserve a network of marine protected areas.

Poverty

The proportion of the Maldives' population living below the national poverty line of USD 1.9 per day decreased from 15 per cent in 2009–2010 to 8.5 per cent in 2016. The most worrying aspect of the poverty is that almost 40 per cent of the 15–24 age group is unemployed, as they reside in rural islands at the end of 2016. The Asian Development Bank reported that 1.5 per cent of employed men earned below USD 1.9 and 1.5 per cent of employed females earned below USD 1.9 per day in 2019, suggesting that the government needs to formulate policies to reduce the falling back of the highly vulnerable nonpoor to poverty alleviation measures.

It is necessary and important to establish an effective social safety net to protect poor families and households from any external shocks, such as Covid-19, SARS, the financial crisis in 2008, or the tsunami in 2005. It is important to note that education and health services are free for all citizens in the Maldives. However, this does not solve the problem of poverty, as the people migrate to the capital city of Malé in search of better living standards. The challenge is to slow rural–urban migration by improving opportunities in the rural areas so that people do not need to migrate to the more developed capital.

Health

The government of the Maldives has made tremendous improvements in the provision of health services for its people in the last few years. The Maldives Health Statistics show that during the period of 2008-2018, the infant mortality rate decreased from 30.8 per cent to 21.3 per cent of 1,000 live births. In 2018, there were 23.6 deaths/1,000 live births among male children and 18.9 deaths/1,000 live births among female children.

The decrease in the maternal mortality ratio is attributed to the wide dispersion of obstetric and other health services to rural areas and the establishment of regional health hubs with access to doctors and nurses skilled in delivery and provision of paternal care. In the past five years, many sustainable development initiatives were implemented to expand the reach of pharmaceutical products by establishing one pharmacy at least in each inhabited island. The Maldives was the first country awarded certification of elimination of malaria, lymphatic filariasis, and measles. The Maldives has implemented many other policies to tackle HIV/AIDS and respiratory diseases.

However, with the change in lifestyle and development, many new health care issues are surfacing with the emergence of chronic noncommunicable diseases. This is mainly due to the morbidity and mortality in the Maldives. The government plan for 2016-2025 identified critical areas and factors, such as living conditions and lifestyle issues, including smoking, unhealthy food in the diet, and obesity. To improve local capacity, the government has invested in training much of the local talent abroad.

Education

One key challenge in achieving the sustainable development goal is raising and improving the quality of education so that teaching capacity can be increased. Providing equal access to primary education for children with special needs is also a significant challenge. The government is committed to implementing education policies and plans to achieve the target ahead of 2030. The policy of No Child Left Behind was implemented so that the delivery of quality education caters to the needs of all children. The Maldives has emphasised a skills-based curriculum with very clearly defined learning outcomes to build competencies required in the twenty-first century. The new curriculum enables students to attain skills and knowledge to promote sustainable lifestyles, human rights, climate change, and global citizenship.

However, the key challenge remains the lack of clear policies, institutions, and systems that will enable and promote lifelong learning and adult education. The current system will require better direction on adult educational pathways, including access to higher-level qualification.

It is important to pay attention to the development of adult education, including education for sustainable development, so as to reskill adults to be more productive and relevant in a changing and volatile economy. The government has emphasised upgrading teachers by ensuring they obtain an undergraduate degree in their profession by 2020. Each teacher is given a scholarship to study for degree programs in the Maldives. The government has also built a Teacher Resource Centre.

One of the initiatives in 2018 was the distribution of iPads to each student in primary and secondary school. During the Covid-19 pandemic, all online sessions are run through online platforms without much issue, suggesting that the initiatives taken are driving the education system to achieve sustainable development goals. The geographically dispersed population in small coral islands adversely affects the cost of provision of educations services.

Governance

To attain sustainable development goals, the government must have effective, accountable, and inclusive institutions at all levels. The Maldives has improved its good governance indicators significantly over the years; this includes additional regulation curbing corruption and ensuring ease of doing business. There are ongoing efforts to strengthen the legal and institutional framework, capacity development, and access to justice. In 2014, the information commissioner's office was established as an independent statutory body. Also, local councils are empowered to contribute and strengthen planning and development at the local level.

The government recognizes the need to strengthen the rule of law so as to increase public confidence in the courts and judicial system. Thus, rule of law and justice remains a primary focus under the good governance sector policy theme of the country's Strategic Action Plan 2009–2013.

Future

Efforts to overcome key challenges and attain sustainable development goals are long-term. The government has significantly improved over the last decade, eradicating absolute poverty and making significant improvement in allowing better access to health services. One of several measures taken was ensuring that every individual has access to educational opportunities.

In public policy, access to clean water and sanitation systems is a priority, and plans must be put in place to ensure sustainable tourism practices. In this regard, the government has recognised the importance of promoting renewable energy and hence has made investments that can make a significant difference in achieving sustainable development goals. Importantly, the government recognises its importance in leading and facilitating this process, and that to do so, good governance must be put in place. This has been the journey of the Maldives so far.

CHAPTER 15

New Normal Behaviours

As the world intensifies its fight against the spread of the Covid-19 pandemic, many governments, industries, and societies are confronting a new normal. Creating a vaccine to combat and treat the infection takes time—months if not years. There is currently no vaccine to cure the disease which has killed more than half a million people as of mid-June 2020, and the figures are expected to rise. This is worrying.

New Normal Routines

Managing daily routines at work, home, and external engagements in the post-pandemic era will be expected to be different. It is very obvious to many who have experienced this period—whether by staying at home or losing someone to the disease—that the coronavirus will teach many new lessons. The majority will be forced to work from home or experience losing a job, and they will realise how fragile society has been and the importance of seeking alternatives to the convenience of the modern lifestyle.

For people in business, this experience has led many to see significant changes to the environment. They have also become aware of how many modern conveniences and markets they may have taken for granted. Some have found that it is not a bad thing to challenge traditional norms. There are more ways technology, for example, can be deployed or exploited to get normal life back on track.

Community Activism

To cope with these challenges, communities will need to question, reassess, and rethink their values, behaviours, and attitudes towards their consumption patterns. Many will have to re-examine the context in which they make decisions. Some basic beliefs and attitudes will be challenged. Managing the new normal in a post-pandemic environment will be a test for most communities.

One of the effects of the lockdown of cities and national borders that led to the closure of economic activities and people movement has been the significant improvement in air pollutions in major cities by as much as 60 per cent, as well in rivers, lakes, and seas, where many have witnessed the return of nature, including schools of dugongs off the seacoast in Thailand.

Climate change has been one of the priorities on the agenda of many developed markets, and this has driven many of their governments' decisions towards a low-carbon economy, including a deliberate policy to phase out coal-powered plants and introduce incentives in favour of electric cars. Elsewhere, there are fresh opportunities to make environmental considerations a new normal when economic planning and development policy are reset.

Consumers can try to make better-informed choices about what products they should buy and really consider the resources that were extracted for that product. While recycling is a standard answer, it does not stop the carbon footprint from increasing. The business community can reduce waste and work to measure and control the pollution that it inflicts on the environment. While big businesses have committed in promises and words, the challenge is translating these principles into measurable action.

Every individual, business, and profession must play a greater role in bringing these strands together and enabling governments, businesses, and consumers to act with due respect for the environment. The United Nations Sustainable Development Goals that were adopted in 2015 must be put at the forefront of the sustainability agenda. There will be opportunities to define a new standard for assessing, measuring, and achieving these targets.

The implications of climate change, if not addressed, are widespread and pose serious and direct threats not only to the global economy and environment but to the basic elements that are essential for life. The most basic of these requirements is a regular supply of water, which is clearly vulnerable to climate change.

For example, a slight increase in temperature in mountainous regions will speed the rate of melting of ice glaciers. This, in turn, will increase the risk of flooding and seriously deplete long-term water supplies, predominantly affecting low-lying communities in the Indian subcontinent, parts of China, and the low-lying areas of the Americas. The loss of a sustainable source of water which feed irrigating rivers, will consequently lead to a decline in crops, with serious implications for communities whose livelihoods and food supplies depend on agriculture. Heat-related deaths and illness will increase, as well as vector-borne diseases like malaria and dengue fever.

Rising sea levels caused by melting polar ice caps will lead to a need for enforced coastal protection, especially for small islands and large coastal cities. Estimates have been made that, within fifty years, around 200 million people could be displaced by rising water levels. Indeed, scientists and industries are now concerned over the recent breakup of ice with a size of 66 square kilometres in the Canada far north that is starting to float towards shipping lanes and oil-drilling regions.

Ecosystems, especially the rich biodiversity of flora and fauna, are especially vulnerable, with 15 to 40 per cent of species facing extinction due to rising temperatures. Studies found that climate change could drive a million of the world's species to extinction by as soon as 2050. Rising temperatures will probably cause regional shifts in weather patterns—the El Nino phenomenon, for example, which has the potential to cause widespread flooding and water shortages.

Although these potentially very serious changes are likely to eventually affect countries all around the world, it is those communities which are the least equipped to deal with them, both economically and structurally, that will be hit first and hardest: the developing world. It is these countries that already struggle with extreme climates and have, on average, higher temperatures and more erratic and heavy rainfall, including monsoon seasons.

Developing countries and communities are, by nature, more dependent on agriculture, which is vulnerable to increasing temperatures or flooding, leading to increased poverty and an inability to be self-sustaining. Experts have predicted that it could affect industries that are essential to many nations, including tourism, agriculture, plantations, property, construction, transport, and fisheries. If sea levels rise as some predict, beaches may retreat up to 100 metres inland, and beach hotels and resorts may disappear. The sea could advance up to 2.5 kilometres inland in some places, causing widespread destruction of agricultural land and facilities.

While rainfall may rise in the region, less water may be available because an expected rise in temperature—up to 3 °C by 2030—will increase the rate of evaporation. At the same time, there will be frequent flash floods in unexpected places. Floods that cause loss of life and destruction to property, and inconvenience thousands of citizens, are just examples of what climate change can do if we are not committed to preventing widespread environmental degradation. The El Nino effect may become even more frequent, and we do not need to be reminded of the terrible hot weather and droughts.

What Can Nations Do?

Several initiatives, treaties, coalitions, and reports have been written and signed over the last twenty years in an attempt to combat the effects of climate change, with varying degrees of success. But still, the world awaits cohesive leadership and concerted international cooperation to facilitate the process and demonstrate the seriousness of commitments, much as some nations have done in their efforts to combat the infectious Covid-19 pandemic.

The new normal of the postpandemic world presents an opportunity for many to refresh and rethink their roles towards the sustainable development agenda, including the battle against climate change. Governments are obliged to fulfil their commitments to public and health policy on environmental challenges and goals. They are also obliged to manage social implications, putting forward a broad range of instruments—including taxes, subsidies, and incentives—across economies. One is to ensure they fulfil the agreement to the global framework to avoid dangerous global warming by limiting global temperature to well below 2 °C, as specified in the 2016 Paris Agreement. They also must pursue efforts to limit it to 1.5 °C. The agreement also aims to strengthen countries' capacity and capability to deal with the adverse impacts of climate change and support them in their efforts.

Governments have played a prominent role in these efforts over the past decades, helping to raise awareness of the importance of sustainability and enacting public polices to require large businesses and governmental bodies to play their part in protecting the environment. Fiscal incentives are important, although low petroleum prices offer distractions and temptations. Because of such issues as use of natural resources, potential polluting activities, and environmental impact, governments must give incentives to pursue renewable energy as part of the new normal. In the words of the *Economist*, action must be taken to consider proper responses to the effects of Covid-19 on the coal industry, for example, by offering opportunities to impede carbonisation.

Industries can and must reassess their reset strategy to include set-aside priorities and encourage companies to explore new and alternative measures which are not based solely on economic profit but also consider longer-term and nonfinancial considerations. These include the extent to which companies operate ethically and with due consideration for the interests of the environment, as well as their own employees and other stakeholders.

Global concerns over plastic pollution in the ocean and elsewhere are recognised as major environmental issues. Videos of rivers clogged with plastics no longer shock the world. Indeed, in and across many emerging countries, rivers continue to be source of water for human consumption, and such social problems harm the livelihood of the poorer segment of the population. Much of the blame is on single-use plastic found in takeaway shopping bags or medication and food containers—more so in the takeaway environment of major cities, where the lifestyle priority is time and convenience. Decades of throwaway culture is not healthy, and much of it has ended up in oceans.

Plastic Waste

Will McCallum, in his book *How to Give Up Plastic*, wrote, 'The problem of plastic pollution is one that affects us all, and therefore one for which we all share responsibility as individuals but also more importantly collectively.' Campaigns to recycle plastics have been in place for many years. Local authorities responsible for the collection may even control the destination of the waste collected. Research has shown that less than half of the items are recollected; the rest is either buried or dumped somewhere. McCallum mentions that 120 billion plastic bottles are made by Coca-Cola annually, 13.9 million tonnes of plastic enter the ocean each year, and 363 million tonnes of plastic are produced each year.

Although the extended lockdown in many cities to curb the spread of the coronavirus outbreak has led to improvement in air pollution, an upsurge in the use of single-use face masks, rubber gloves, and plastic bottles of sanitiser risk an increase in plastic waste not properly disposed of. Environmentalists have warned that the lack of responsibility on the part of users will worsen the global fight against plastic pollution.

Consumers

Consumers can and should make a difference in the new normal by being better informed on the source of the products they want to purchase or consume, as much are these are now disclosed. Reducing individual plastic footprint should be another behaviour for the new normal. One example is for consumers to consider giving up plastic in the household completely. While it is easy to replace plastic bags, it may not be so for food storage. But there are now substitutes or alternatives to the so-called convenience plastics have offered. Consumers can play a significant part in reducing the global plastic footprint.

Plastic will not disappear overnight, but it is important to mitigate the threat of plastic to the future of planet. The reduction in the consumption of plastics will have a positive effect on downstream activities, including sustaining the marine life that is also a source of food for people in many parts of the world.

Alternatives

In the postpandemic era, debates will surface on alternative uses of energy to support transportation. Reducing the carbon footprint will resurface as a priority. One of these issues will centre on technology as an alternative to the way people and businesses get connected and participate across business and social engagements. During the major lockdowns, working from home using digital channels increased by many folds, creating greater opportunities to reduce the carbon footprint through less demand for travel and related costs.

Businesses are well placed to continue their efficiency drive. Many will be forced to accelerate work-from-home practices, use less physical space, and manage health risks.

All of these are positive towards climate action. There will be rethinking on the use of sustainable practices as part of a new normal way of managing risks.

It was not long ago that reports on carbon emissions showed an increase. Protecting the planet and its natural resources is a concern that affects us all and which calls upon us all to consider how we can help. It is ironic that it has taken a global pandemic with a huge loss of life to show world leadership that pandemics and climate are global concerns, and such matters must be taken seriously.

Although the new digital era will be marked by increased distractions, the battle to slow down global warming must not abate. Transitions to new normal behaviours demand a rethink of public policies, practices, and attitudes.

CHAPTER 16

Youth

There is no doubt that the youth population in any nation forms the backbone of the country's future and relevance. According to United Nations statistics, the world's youth population is roughly 1.8 billion, representing a quarter of the world's growing population. However, 90 per cent of these youths, between ages of 10 and 24, live in less-developed countries. The United Nations recognises the strategic importance of these youths across the seventeen sustainable development goals (SDGs) of 2030, designed to tackle the global concerns of eradicating youth unemployment, gender discrimination, poverty, income inequality, and climate change.

The platform of the Partnership for SDGs is open to all stakeholders—including member states, civil society, local authorities, private sector, scientific and technological community, academia, and others—to register a voluntary commitment or multistakeholder partnership which aims to drive the implementation of the 2030 agenda and the seventeen SDGs and to provide periodic updates on progress.

An issue of *World Youth Report*, a flagship publication of the United Nations, identified several key challenges and opportunities. One of the key challenges facing youths today is the uncertainty of a guaranteed job beyond education. Youth unemployment has been a massive issue in the least-developed nations. In some places, it can be as high as 40 per cent.

In response to the challenges, the UN 2030 agenda is designed to include youth participation. The philosophy is that youth involvement would not be ignored or understated. Young people represent a larger proportion of the global population, and if there are better opportunities, the influence of the youths of today would be ideal.

Employment

Today, one of the uncertainties facing youths is the changing nature of work, made worse by the disappearance of traditional jobs, many of which have been replaced by automation and technology. Manufacturing, hospitality services, banking, and mining are among the fields that have undergone massive transformation. Greater efficiency through automation and the increasing use of artificial intelligence means fewer opportunities at the entry level and less demand for new skills.

Youth unemployment has been identified as one of the biggest challenges. Indeed, it was estimated that a total of 600 million new jobs would need to be created in the next fifteen years to absorb youths entering the job market. Today, social entrepreneurship is a sustainable job creator. There is a strong belief that social entrepreneurship is not only in line with the preferences of young people but enables them to become agents of change.

Importantly, a key takeaway from these programmes includes the agenda for Sustainable Development (SD) 2030, with a strong emphasis on education, job opportunities, and contemporary issues. The SD 2030 agenda is an opportunity for the youths of today not only to understand the sustainability mission but also to ensure that their combined future of economic, social, and ecological development is not compromised.

It is recognised that youths do have some challenges in coping with a fast-changing world, but they also have different challenges and needs. The youth movement has no shortage of ideas and issues, but they experience differences in terms of their own accessibility to opportunities, resources, and education.

Youth Activism

Youth movements have been recognised as important stakeholders. There are already in place hundreds of international and local agencies devoting resources to raising the capacity of youth as well as improving their awareness on a broad range of sustainability matters and engagements. Targeted at young people across the world, especially those from the least-developed countries, millions of dollars have been spent on activities that have a primary focus of empowering youths to be better managers in environmental or social development matters.

A number of these policy recommendations are being tabled at different levels. There is no shortage of issues being addressed, and many affect youth. The United Nations Conference on Trade and Development's annual youth forum has key issues affecting youth at the forefront; these include employment trends, technological disruptions, and entrepreneurship. While the biannual event brings out relevant issues and solutions, it gives important inputs from the youth movement to the world investment forum.

There is already in place a platform at the UN which allows diverse stakeholders to commit voluntarily in multistakeholder partnerships to the 2030 sustainable development goals. Managed by the UN Department of Economic and Social Affairs, the platform has brought together many stakeholders to work on common issues. NEXUS is one example. A nonprofit organisation, NEXUS went international in 2011 to focus on philanthropic activities. It has since grown and expanded its presence across every continent, leading conferences, research, and awareness campaigns on contemporary matters including social investment, charity work, disaster recovery, and climate change. NEXUS as a network has turned into a million-dollar organisation helping youths in start-ups and charity work across diverse societies.

Such enthusiasm and energy have also been demonstrated by young people participating in joint actions at the annual World Economic Forum at Davos. One of these was the founding of the Global Shapers Community, a network of activists, technologists, and entrepreneurs under 30. The community has already enrolled more than 8,000 members across more than 160 countries. Since its founding, the network has carried out projects on disaster rescue and recovery, and more recently on climate change. Various individuals have worked at the grassroots level to raise awareness of gender issues as well education on skills, health, and minority challenges.

More impactful among the youth is a 17-year-old Swede by the name of Greta Thunberg. Her climate speech on 'Our lives are in your hands' outside the Swedish parliament inspired and attracted worldwide attention. Her brief scolding of government leaders at the UN General Assembly in New York on 23 September 2019 received global attention. Her three words of 'How dare you' in her speech made quite an impact on the international stage, especially her comments on companies that are more concerned with profitability than the impact of their operations on the community, customers, and employees. Although Greta Thunberg targeted the thrust of her climate speech on carbon budgets and time concerns, she has also set her eyes on Western governments.

There is much more to do if the youth movement is to make others take notice and become more involved. Studies involving thousands of young individuals identified environment, human resources, fair business practices, community involvement, products, ethics, and corruption as primary concerns. In a recent survey conducted by the Sustainable Development Policy Institute on key challenges facing youth in South Asia countries, the importance of employment, policy discourse, and possible options to promote youth employment were highlighted.

Based on the interviews conducted with a selected group, there was strong importance and emphasis placed on employability of youths, as well as a recognition of the required skills and options available for them. Such observation was consistent elsewhere: there was a concern over youth unemployment and equal opportunities and access to work. The importance of inclusive employment was covered in one of the SDGs, with an emphasis on 'promoting sustained, inclusive, and sustainable growth, full and productive employment, and decent work for all'. It is a norm among many governments that youths be given the opportunity to acquire relevant skills and opportunities to maximise their potential.

Interestingly, a recent study conducted by British-based Prince's Trust showed that 57 per cent of 16- to 25-year-olds believe that social media has created undue pressure on them to succeed. More than a third of the young community surveyed believed they would never be as happy as their peers online. The findings of a few studies on the challenges the complexity of issues will require are helpful when it comes to embracing sustainability principles. Some may argue, however, that given limited resources, there are other prioritises.

Change and Awareness

External drivers of change that are of immediate concern to youth development and challenges are understanding expectations of youths from diverse backgrounds. Developed markets are quicker to understand new demands to embrace sustainability, transparency, and commitments than, say, developing or least-developed markets, which are grappling with other economic, social, and political demands.

While there are growing demands to demonstrate higher social and environmental standards, youths in the least-developed markets will have other challenges. Political freedom of expression and opportunities may also differ. One commonality is that convergence of technology and social media has reduced knowledge gaps, and it is also fair to say, for example, that digital lifestyles are no different across national boundaries.

There are issues around such social matters as discrimination based on gender, race, and religion that youths openly discuss, and opinions are expressed quite freely across the channels. The recent case of George Floyd, who died at the hands of police, ignited and motivated thousands of youths to protest on the streets across many cities in the United States, as well as in London, Sydney, Brazil, and elsewhere. Youths are protesting against racism as well as voicing support for racial diversity. They are calling out to the establishment to make a change.

Stakeholder Commitment

An important process is getting commitments from those with greater influence to embrace their responsibility so that a trickle-down effect will bring relevant stakeholders together. The journey of youth involvement in wanting social change is an uneasy one. There are, however, businesses that may feel any change means additional commitments and these additional costs will be unnecessary burdens on them. But it is important that business and society do feel an obligation to sustain the new generation that will bring benefits to all.

Regulators are also advocating to small- to medium-size enterprises (SMEs) for a sustainable future where community development and welfare do not come at the expense of short-term profits. Recent high-profile cases of ecological damage and site accidents that have resulted in the loss of lives and property not only drive home the message that sustainability issues are very relevant to SMEs but that failure to address such concerns is a threat to both business and local society.

It is increasingly evident that sustainability is an important part of the business environment. It is a commitment to do good business in a manner that will not only contribute to economic development but also improve the quality of life of the workforce, the local community, and society at large.

International Youth Day on August 12 symbolises the recognition given to the importance and potential of youth by the United Nations. Numerous initiatives have already taken place. One example is the role of youth in combating the world's challenge of eradicating poverty as part of sustainable development. With this in mind, the theme of poverty and responsible consumption was launched, reminding youth that the repercussions of excessive consumption would not be in line with the sustainability concept. By inculcating habits of responsible consumption and empowering youth with the right capacity and skills, there is a strong belief that youth can be encouraged to reduce waste and even embrace the concept of recycling and reusing. There are already great examples of youth initiatives, from recycling and food packing to development of travel applications, all of which fit into the sustainability agenda that gives priority to environmental stewardship and skill development.

The mission of the United Nations–driven Sustainable Development Solution Network is to drive and promote the implementation of SDGs through education, research, policy analysis, and global cooperation. One example of these activities took place in Indonesia, home to 60 million youth, where many initiatives have been taken not only on the promotion of sustainability concepts but also to build capacity and capability development among the local youths. The implementation is not without challenges for a diverse country with many developmental challenges. But more than half of the initiatives are already being implemented in line with national development priorities, which are to ensure youths are equipped with future skills and mindsets within the context of sustainable development. Such example ought to be applauded and encouraged elsewhere.

CHAPTER 17

Education

Education for sustainable development (ESD) has gained much traction since its inception. It is hard to disagree with the noble intent and objectives of ESD. It is one of the necessary drivers towards the achievement of UN sustainable development goals (SDGs). It is not just about raising environmental awareness; the intent is to empower people to make informed decisions, taking into consideration the bigger picture of making society a better place to live for present and future generations.

UNESCO defines ESD as addressing elements of climate issues; ecology and biodiversity; consumption; income inequality; gender equality; and human rights. Not all mainstream education contains such specified topics but a far-reaching change in the way education is being addressed, redesigned, and delivered.

Education is a key part of the sustainability movement. It is complex and time-consuming, involving the participation of a multiplicity of stakeholders. There is also the challenge of re-orientating education with sustainability principles and perspectives that require inputs from a host of multiple but often diverse stakeholders. There must be buy-in not just from policymakers but from users and consumers as well. Incorporating the important elements of sustainability for educational purpose depends on detailed attention being paid to issues, ensuring compatibility with national relevance and aspirations.

Not all may agree to the full suite of SDGs. There will be hard choices to be made at the national and local levels. But if ESD is to be realised by the year 2030, there is a need to integrate the important elements of the seventeen SDGs into education, especially in the areas of health, education, poverty, energy, resources, and economic security.

Purpose and Goals

ESD, targeted at youths and schoolchildren, is aimed at encouraging collaborative learning. The learning objectives are to allow students to think differently and apply what they've learned towards a sustainable future. The ESD for 2030 framework developed by UNESCO allows every single student to connect the dotted lines between the economic, social, and environmental impacts of human activities. These involve transferring know-how, empowering, and building capacity and applications for adaptation to diverse situations and cases.

Not all may be in the national interest, and these may be perceived to be against national priorities, where it is not uncommon to find challenges ranging from fossil fuel dependence to gender issues. There are also the challenges of human rights abuses at workplaces and development issues involving ancestral rights and so on. These social and environmental issues and conflicts reinforce the fragile and rich diversity of interests on the planet, but the opportunities are available to address questions on costs and conflicts between development, profits, and environment. Bigger issues on climate change, social pressures, and the growing disparity between societies may be more acceptable, but they are by no means acceptable to all in terms of content and objectives.

These issues have not gone away even during the global pandemic, during which one could observe the extent of economic damage in many nations as governments scrambled to prevent the coronavirus infection. As of June 2020, more than 5 million people have been infected, and more than 400,000 have died. The lockdown of national borders and cities has posed real dilemmas for poor nations faced with the difficult choice of closing down economic activities versus taking a risk by allowing many poor people to earn their daily wages.

There is little disagreement over economic impacts that have caused loss of jobs and closure of businesses, but from an ecological perspective, researchers have noticed that there has been a more than 40 per cent decrease in air pollution across the major cities of London, New York, New Delhi, and Beijing.

Learning

One of the UN's SDGs is education. Its agenda is to ensure 'inclusive and equitable quality education and promote lifelong learning opportunities for all'. ESD represents a broad spectrum of areas where common indicators include level of access, literacy level, quality of knowledge, and gender opportunities.

Education has a far-reaching impact on values and attitudes being shaped towards a sustainable society. It is necessary, at least from the way society is to be governed, measured, and managed. It is essential and desirable at different levels, including both formal and informal education and learning. For many, education leads to a more tolerant quality of life, where nature and humans could coexist. For this to be sustained over many generations, the development and acquisition of sustainability knowledge and skills are necessary and must be accessible to all.

Towards this end, ESD curriculum language must embrace the whole spectrum of the triple-bottom-line languages of economic, environment, and social responsibilities. Learning and education in sustainability will invoke a series of debates with civil societies and partners, including different thoughts, imaginations, and opinions on the what to and the how to, especially on the processes, trends, and developments in the use of pedagogy and tools, plus market economics and social preferences. Towards this end, there are principles of governance and ethics that must be understood, embraced, and put into practice.

There is, however, a view that learning methods that are more participative, experiential, and engaging have a better chance of success. The success factors are also to ensure clear differences in both thinking and expressing. The approaches in the future of learning in a sustainable space will see such key elements given emphasis. These include a demand for greater collaboration and sharing of experiences through case studies.

A majority of experts will agree that advances in technology in the digital era will shape and determine the quality and amount of what people learn, develop, educate, and apply across many possibilities as societies advance.

There are now choices beyond what one can imagine, allowing people to pick and choose how to learn or educate and how and where to apply these. Such choices are decided in a variety of ways.

Empowering

It is part of the ESD agenda that education is all about inclusivity. It must be participatory in teaching and learning methods so as to motivate and empower learners to change their behaviour and take necessary action in the context of sustainable development. The underlying principle is that no one is to be left behind. UNESCO defines this as allowing access at all levels.

To put it in a sustainability context, a reorientation of education will allow people to acquire skills, know-how, values on ethics and governance, and motivation necessary for addressing climate and sustainability issues in a collaborative way. UNESCO to date has already engaged more than a million teachers in more than 50 countries. More than 500 business schools have signed on to the Principles for Responsible Management Education developed by the UN Global Compact.

Building Capacity

The success criteria of educating sustainability requires the acquisition of leadership competencies, including the ability to do scenario planning and gain a big-picture understanding of the challenges of confronting a planet to accommodate possibly a population of more than 10 million by the turn of the century. Not only that, it is about the ability to sustain and ensure a balance between the continuing exploitation of resources against the possible severe repercussions of ecological damage to climate disruptions. Already, the United Nations is predicting a no-change scenario of 3 billion people subject to hot and dry weather by 2070. Such challenges will demand that every member state of the United Nations ensure preparedness in terms of its capacity to adapt, a policy that drives a zero-carbon agenda and ensures adequate capacity at all levels, including education, learning, and training.

There are already concerted efforts internationally towards sustainable development on education, and the number of pedagogy tools has grown exponentially. It is a well-known observation that technology has brought about fundamental and structural change to the way people learn and contribute. Studies have shown that technology improves productivity in the learning space. Digital learning tools—from tablets and laptops to hand-held mobile phones—have enabled courses to run 24/7.

Such connected leaning has enabled flexibility and self-management. Courses now can be recorded, and students can learn at their own pace or choose a more interactive option when courses go live. The transformation of learning over the past three decades has improved not only productivity for providers but, for the learners, a new source of motivation and empowerment.

The acceleration of such learning experiences has shaped and expanded the global reach of education and learning providers. Hence, from an economic perspective, it has reduced the cost of delivery and made better use of time for both learners and teachers. As learning institutions and individuals continue to innovate and embrace the technology of the future for the education system, there are challenges ahead.

Technology Transfer

The drive for more online learning can be observed from the recent lockdown of cities to combat the spread of Covid-19 infections. To begin with, thousands of schools and institutions of higher learning around the world had to be shut to prevent the spread of infection. This did not bring the learning process to a halt; instead, there was an immediate upsurge in the number of courses that went online, from webinars to virtual live instruction that ran across easy-to-use platforms. The return of virtual classroom training can be equally engaging and productive, but online delivery channels have become the strategic driver, as well as part of risk management, which many institutions may not have regarded it as before.

Artificial intelligence (AI) has already made rapid advancements in industry, and more so in the digital economy. AI has successfully helped humans connect with computers. Extensive AI research towards improving cognitive functions in robot ability to reason and explain will be the next shape of things to come. Such a revolution will be part of technological advancement. There would be no stopping robots with the help of AI to learn on the job, teach, and even reason, to name a few possibilities.

AI is already being used in classrooms and included as part of innovations. There is little doubt this will change the learning style and habits of the future. The advancement made with AI is not only helping students but helping institutions with administrative services, research, and developments. The challenge is whether robots will one day replace teachers.

Research-Backed Education

The future of learning in a sustainable world has been professionally researched. One of the impacts of technology in learning in recent years has been its capacity to enable close collaborations and connectedness among users. Students and learners can now reach out to each other in their learning activities, borderless and 24/7. This has allowed better partnership and facilitated richer experiences from truly diverse ethnicities and geographies.

Indeed, technology has given learning communities unlimited opportunities to learn and grow. It has created a knowledge-based world in which access to information is easy and fast. These developments have given almost every single individual opportunities, ideas, and connections that can be adapted and customised to each community's specified needs.

The educators of the future will likely focus on analytics and adaptation to suit different needs and wants. The inclusive nature of the approach underlines the importance of interdisciplinary skills, ensuring communications across all languages in understanding and influencing behaviours towards raising standards and know-how. A central piece to strengthen this goal is not only to increase the supply of able teachers but also to equip them with devices within an ecosystem that allows innovation in teaching capabilities, access to know-how, and the means to connect to relevant partners and other stakeholders.

The Future Is Here

The future of learning is already here. In the digital age, new technologies are already changing every aspect of our society. Technology will be a leading driver of all new value created in the digital era. There are opportunities to acquire AI-enabled system to innovate learning as well as taking advantage of the interdependency towards realisation of SDGs.

Such developments and opportunities are well supported by the World Economic Forum (WEF), where hundreds of influential political and business leaders meet annually in Davos, Switzerland. The WEF highlighted the role education can and should play in advancing goals of sustainable development. One example where WEF sees real opportunity is in public health, food security, and energy. WEF sees education as the means to shift the way people think, act, and discharge their responsibilities towards the common goal of realising sustainable development.

A strong education system is one in which institutions such as universities can enlarge their level of influence through providing opportunities for research and innovations, skill acquisition, and community development. Universities have all the existing infrastructure to ensure that this opportunity to make a difference through education is maximised. They are well positioned to forge greater partnerships to deliver greater good.

The sustainability future is already here. The digital age will see acceleration of new virtual learning environments that are more accessible and convenient to achieve a wider reach and yet are affordable for many. The effects of these on ESD for sustainable development will be positive. The challenge is whether the sustainable development goals of 2030 will be realised sooner or later. That is left to be seen.

CHAPTER 18

Risks

A BBC report on 14 January 2020 predicted that the Australian forest fires would become normal on a warmer planet. This is not only worrying but a massive risk to all its inhabitants. The massive bush fires in the states of New South Wales and Victoria are the largest and deadliest the world has ever experienced, surpassing recent fires in the Amazon, Siberia, and California.

The Australian fires destroyed 18.6 million hectares of forest. Twenty-nine lives were lost, and a Sydney local newspaper estimated that 480 million animals in the state of New South Wales perished. An area almost the size of Belgium, or at least twenty times the size of Tokyo, was burned to the ground.

In response, a group of scientists in the United Kingdom was quick to warn global policymakers of what the world would be like if future global warming reaches an increase of 3 °C. Studies have shown a clear link between climate change and severe drought, which comes with a potent combination of prolonged high temperatures and forest fires plus a host of ecological and health issues.

Moment of Crisis

The world's famous natural historian, Sir David Attenborough, described the recent Australian forest fire as 'the moment of crisis has come'. In his interview with the BBC, he said, 'We have been putting things off for year after year, and there are urgent steps to take, simply because the temperatures of the earth are rising.'

Signs of an unwell planet are increasingly visible these days. What took place in Australia is not a stand-alone situation. There have been frequent recurrences of such extreme weather conditions reported throughout Europe, America, Asia, and the African subcontinent. There are now fears these weather extremes will become more frequent and common, especially during the summer on both continents. Each time, the intensity of the drought gets worse.

These concerns resonate with warnings from experts at the series of United Nations Climate Change Conferences, where they warned governments that extreme weather is a direct result of climate change, the effects are irreversible, and the consequences can be damaging. Climate change, caused principally by large-scale emissions of industrial gases such as carbon dioxide (CO_2), is to some experts the greatest threat humankind has ever faced, because the consequences will threaten the habitability of the earth.

The risks confronting global communities of regulators, policymakers, businesses, and individuals are not just extreme hot weather. There are already signs that weather conditions will become harder to predict, and critics are expecting the worst. It is not difficult to see why. Reports of fast rapid disintegration of the ice shelf in the Arctic suggest such an alarming rate that we can now expect the summer sea ice to disappear in less than ten years' time.

The vast Arctic cap has for centuries served as a reflection for sunlight, preventing overheating of the planet. Repercussions of its disappearance include greater absorption of the sun's energy and hence more warming of the earth. The warming of the sea and rising sea level spells danger and trouble for the majority of the planet's inhabitants.

Worrying Developments

The disappearance of the great ice sheets of the Antarctic is most worrying. Scientists are convinced that this is the cause of frequent weather extremes. For the first time, humans have an influence over the climate system. Scientists are also convinced that centuries of burning of fossil fuels to meet the global consumption of the ever-increasing human population, especially during the postwar era, has accelerated the pumping of carbon dioxide into the atmosphere.

With the earth getting a lot more crowded—world population, according to the United Nations Population Division, is expected to increase from the current 7 billion to 9.2 billion by 2050, an increase of 2.5 billion, the equivalent of the world population in 1950—world leaders now have a massive challenge on their hands. The concentration of greenhouse gas has already jumped to a record high in 2018 and shows no signs of decreasing, according to the Global Carbon Project. The authors of the report have concluded that the emission trend can still be turned around if there are cuts made in the high-energy sectors of transport, industry, and farming.

At the global level, most sceptics do not believe that the Paris Agreement, which challenges all nations to pursue the goal of limiting global temperature increase to well below 2 °C, will work. The Intergovernmental Panel on Climate Change's worst-case scenario is that global temperature will rise by up to 6.4 per cent by 2100. Developed nations should shoulder much of the blame, since the richest 7 per cent of the world's population is responsible for half of all CO_2 emissions, although China, Brazil, and India have doubled their CO_2 emissions over the past ten years. Today, the United States, China, Russia, and Japan are responsible for half of all CO_2 emissions.

International communities, while acknowledging the need to overcome these global problems, so far have committed to contain the rise to no more than 2 per cent. Many have yet to produce real serious action on reducing greenhouse gas emissions into the atmosphere. The Madrid climate conference in 2019 did succeed in convincing government heads to recognise the threats of climate change, but whether the respective governments have the will to carry out their commitments by the year 2030 is left to be seen.

There are enough road maps to offer each of the member countries plans to pursue reduction of carbon emission by as much as 25 to 40 per cent, but the challenge is winning support from the larger polluters—the United States, Russia, and China. There are risks that with the world experiencing trade wars and a tougher economic environment, the climate change agenda will not be a matter of urgency. Indeed, many legislators, especially in the smaller nations, are expected to face resistance to any change to the high-carbon lifestyle if the addiction to a fossil fuel–driven society and lifestyle is not addressed.

Despite all the actions taken, there are experts who believe that nations should be prepared for the massive risks warmer weather will create across continents. Agriculture will be the first sector to be hit, as soaring temperatures make land impossible to plough—worse still in many areas of the world where people are already poor and hungry. More than 50 per cent of water is devoted to sustaining agricultural activities, and any reduction can only mean that countries in central Asia, southern Europe, and Australia will experience longer dry spells, leading to political tensions and violence. Food security becomes very vulnerable and poses threats to the political and social stability of any nation.

Climate Migration

Climate change resulting in prolonged droughts and flooding will have a particularly negative impact on the African and South Asia continents. More than 100 million people will be under threat, creating huge problems of large-scale climate migration. Even incidents of starvation are set to rise if food production is wiped out On these continents. In such an event, political and diplomatic solutions may not be enough to prevent escalation of possible border wars between nations.

The harmful consequences of climate change are indeed unimaginable. Yet many governments have little direction as to what they are expected to do to combat it. Europeans, while being the most vocal about climate change, have not succeeded in approaching their Paris emissions target. At the same time, large investments have gone into the development of renewable energy technology and adaptation technologies.

Reminders

Given such vulnerabilities, it is not surprising that on the World Economic Forum Global Risks Perception Survey, environmental concerns received the highest ratings. The extreme weather concern includes risks such as water stress; long periods of drought and forest fires; and tropical storms and flooding. All this adverse weather is a risk factor, and in guarding the level of investment, business leaders are now better informed of the adverse impacts to their assets, as well as the sustainability of their markets.

On the other hand, in some places, frequent flooding can put more pressure on sewage systems, causing a drop in the quality of drinking water and a threat to public health that can possibly bring a pandemic that wreaks havoc on any health system. Urban infrastructures will also face potential threats from the devastation of extreme weather, such as Hurricane Katrina, which hit New Orleans not too long ago.

In low-lying areas, sea level will continue to rise by as much as 60 centimetres, threatening coastal communities and coral reefs. Rising sea levels will destroy substantial coastal areas in low-lying countries such as Bangladesh at the very moment when their populations are mushrooming. Melting ice, according to experts, can create changes in ocean circulation, resulting in warming and increased absorption of CO_2. That is bad for aquatic habitats, posing huge threats to the fishing industry and its supporting industries. A quarter of the world's coral reef will disappear. Indeed, the Great Barrier Reef of Australia will be one of the first casualties should global warming continue at its current rate.

There are few doubts over the high risks associated with climate change. There is enough scientific evidence to demonstrate the moral and just case of taking action now. It is not only government legislation that is necessary but business and industry ensuring their survival through environmental sustainability. Consumers too can play their part through a change in their shopping habits.

Unless sustainability changes are escalated, the war against climate change may be over before it even begins. The Covid-19 pandemic has reminded us what the world would be like if human-led activities stop. With a reported reduction in air and ocean pollution, nature has returned somewhat, but many observers would regard this as only temporary. Nonetheless, it has reminded governments of the risk of climate change that has not gone away.

Both governments and business communities must see these weather risks as real dangers to their existence, present and future. Many have started their contributions from reduction of fossil fuels to the use of biodegradable materials. While they may see this as a way of giving back to society, the reality is that greenhouse gas reduction targets may not be met. While there are governments which intend to reduce CO_2 emissions by at least half by 2050, many more are waiting to see how this will turn out before making their commitments. When they come to their senses and see that something must be done, it will be too late.

CHAPTER 19

Attitudes

To overcome sustainability challenges, there must be concerted efforts among the 7 billion people on earth to embrace today's buzzword: the *new normal*. It involves a commitment to discard old conveniences, embrace new habits and attitudes, and develop the habit of using the resources sustainably and responsibly in everyday life. The authors of *The Future We Choose*, Christiana Figueres and Tom Rivett-Carnac, have described it as a necessary action to 'let go of the old world'.

To ensure shared responsibility, it is necessary to motivate behavioural change, defined by appropriate actions taken and attitudes changed towards the broad sustainability agenda: a change in one's emotional reaction towards the three interconnected matters of ecology, economy, and society. Changing mindsets is one thing. Others include awareness, acceptance, and actions necessary to embrace the change.

Changing attitudes and behaviours is a lengthy process, often complex. It may be unrealistic to expect everyone to embrace one common policy. But movement for a common cause often will invoke public reaction, especially on issues that affect the public and society.

One may recall the thousands who protested air pollution in New York way back in 1966. More recently, in late summer 2018, there were street protests that called for the government to do more against climate change. When a 16-year-old Greta Thunberg decided to go on strike in front of the Swedish parliament in August 2018, her action went viral, which started a movement for action against climate change. Her actions as a teenage girl gained enough global publicity to persuade many corporate leaders that climate change as a sustainability issue had to be taken more seriously.

Equally persuasive was the immediate reaction to the forest fires in the Amazon and in Australia. Public reactions are often of empathy or strong feelings of disapproval. Not many, however, would go higher than the feeling of injustice or sorrow about environmental destruction.

Pandemic Impact

The outbreak of Covid-19 that inflicted damage on major economies and communities has brought about several changes in terms of attitudes and behaviours. As of September 2020, a total of 30 million cases have been recorded, and more than 900,000 have died from the infectious disease. While it does not look like the virus is going away anytime soon, millions are resigned to the fact that the future looks more uncertain, and health issues have gained much attention and should be treated as a priority.

As a result of lockdowns in many cities, scientists are reporting clearer skies and fresher air. There are temporary respites on the environment, as emission of carbon has been drastically reduced through thousands of planes being grounded, highways free of normal heavy traffic in almost every city, and smog disappearing due to the shutdown of factories. In Venice, it was reported that water in the canals saw a return of fish and even dolphins. Many fishing fleets also sat idle, leading to a drop in demand. The industry has now turned bearish.

The reduction in economic activities is seen to be temporary; hence a view that the decline in global carbon emission is also temporary. Indeed, the International Energy Agency has cautioned that the momentum towards a push for green policies may be slowed, delaying a possible realisation of sustainable development goals.

Going Digital

The Covid-19 pandemic has triggered a series of effects beyond the expectations of many. The world saw an immediate rise in the use of videoconferencing to an all-time high. Business in all major markets sought alternative digital means to connect, meet, and engage during the lockdown of major cities. The shift to online meetings and transactions is apparent, as working from home became mainstream overnight.

IT magazine reports that both Microsoft and Google enjoyed a jump in the number of downloads, and Zoom enjoyed such healthy growth that the estimated net worth of its founder went up by more than USD 4 billion. The changes in work style are likely to stay for a while, as the world waits for a vaccine or at least for things to be safe enough for many to travel. It is likely that many governments, businesses, and individuals may decide that such habits are equally as efficient as and safer than working in an office, and there is a strong possibility that a shifts away from transport will take place.

Social isolation is one scenario that no sustainability planners would like to consider, but the pandemic has forced behavioural change that is hard to ignore. So long as the pandemic continues to pose a public health risk, it is highly likely that social isolation practices will become the acceptable norm across all walks of life. One wonders whether such behaviours will become permanent once the pandemic is over.

Change Is Hard

One reason embracing sustainability practices will not be easy, despite the lessons to be learnt from the pandemic experience, is that change is not easy. There will be unintended consequences from the current delivery system. Take, for example, the use of plastic packaging for delivery services. Demand for online delivery services spiked during the lockdown in cities. Shariffa Sabrina, founder of PEKA, an environmental nongovernmental organisation based in Kuala Lumpur, said the following to local newspaper the *Star*:

> Getting meals has become more convenient as it is literally at your fingertips. However, it involves a lot of single-use plastic packaging, which of course is damaging to the environment as most end up in rivers and oceans. As companies that profit from such activities, they have a responsibility to ensure that their activities are sustainable and do not harm the environment.

Something similar was seen in Thailand, a country which was proud to impose a ban on single-use plastic just before the pandemic outbreak. During the one-month city lockdown, plastic waste soared by 62 per cent. Reuters reported that this was made up of mostly plastic wrapping and packaging for food deliveries and online shopping. As a result, the country is poised to maintain its position as one of the top four plastic polluters of the ocean. As much as 3,432 tonnes of plastic waste are thrown away in the capital city, including plastic bags, containers, bottles, and cups, all of which are waste generated by a throwaway society.

For decades, major economies have thrived on consumer-driven growth. The years of high street retail growth have led to an increase in the use of resources from plastic packaging to delivery. One example is the clothing giant Primark. Based in the United Kingdom, the high street retailer makes RM 650 million in sales per month, according to a BBC report on 21 April 2020. But the unintended consequence of the production and packaging is an increase in waste that ultimately leads to more carbon emissions, pressure on land use and deforestation, and eventually climate change.

The Covid-19 pandemic may have temporarily forced many retailers to close, but the social consequences of unemployment among young people and a sluggish economy are unacceptable to governments. Consumer demand for apparel and lifestyle products is an inevitable part of economic growth. There are now companies devoted to the sustainability movement that have combined their business model with production of goods that are made to be more socially and environmentally responsible.

Eco-Friendly

Such a change of attitudes is driven by shifting consumer preferences towards an eco-friendlier brand. One example is Timberland. The forty-plus-year-old retailer has a responsibility promise that embraces sustainability principles and values. The company did a survey among 1,000 men and women to define its top sustainable behaviours, which include supporting environmental causes, conserving water, recycling, and understanding the importance of sustainability.

Many will recognise that for global economies to flatten the curve of carbon emissions, the release of greenhouse gases must be reduced. Limiting growth to 2 °C is not going to happen, according to leading scientists. Changing human attitudes, values, and behaviours will not be easy. People are not convinced of the dangers of climate change, rising sea levels, water stress, or even plastic waste, and they do not understand how these will affect them.

Perhaps to overcome this pessimism, we should demand greater action, the same way some governments effectively tackled the dreadful effects of the Covid-19 pandemic. The question is, should the global community only react when disaster strikes? But there is hope.

One might recall the Extinction Rebellion protest in London, which started in May 2018 when a group of one hundred academics called for action support against climate change. Whether this will bring about a zero-emission society in the United Kingdom has received serious attention. The government has promised that its climate change committee will publish its own plan on how the country can battle global warming.

Behaviours and Attitudes

There are already pockets of change in attitudes, from buying habits right down to deliberate government policies and practices. Changing consumer behaviours takes time, but surveys consistently show that the average person would be happy to take additional steps to make a difference. Large retailers such as Walmart are already committed to the promotion of sustainability, including its own supply chain management. In terms of waste, there is already technology available to allow recycling and reuse of plastic materials.

Changing attitudes will nonetheless require a combination of public awareness and reminders, education, enforcement of government policies, and obtaining everyone's cooperation. Efforts must make it simple for all to do the right thing but hard or expensive to do the wrong thing. This will be the challenge. Persuading people to discard conveniences takes time. For attitudes and preferences to change, there must be both incentives and deterrents.

CHAPTER 20

Convergence

The overwhelming evidence produced by the scientific, environmental, and media communities leaves very few people in doubt that the sustainability dangers of poverty, health concerns, climate change, pollution, deforestation, plastic waste, and social inequalities are real. The combination of such challenges is daunting. To overcome these significant threats, there must be a convergence of efforts within this and coming decades. Recognising that these threats are overlapping, the question becomes whether the current global leadership has the capacity to overcome these challenges and whether goals and deadlines can be met.

One clue to answering this is to observe how global leadership and communities coped with the potentially serious threat to humanity posed by the Covid-19 pandemic. The infectious disease, with no vaccine in sight yet, has already infected more than 30 million worldwide. Equally devastating, more than 900,000 people have died as of September 2020.

One scenario posed is that if the global temperature continues to rise at the same rate as in recent years, then in the not-too-distant future, the earth will be much hotter. With that comes severe consequences for both developed and developing countries. Many may not be confident enough to agree to the Paris climate goal of keeping the earth's warming to no more than 2 °C. But climate change has already taken place, and it will over time lead to rising sea levels that will bring misery to millions living in coastal areas.

Some places will experience prolonged droughts. Already there are fears that warming of the oceans is threatening the reproductive capabilities of fish species and eventually humanity. These scenarios suggest the possible emergence of climate disruption that will lead to more geopolitical tension between nations.

The dangerous consequences of sustainability concerns will affect every society and community. It is the obligation and responsibility of a diverse range of stakeholders—from governments, businesses, and civil society organizations to individuals—to adopt all sorts of innovations to promote responsible and sustainable consumption and production. It is, after all, in their interest to protect their future, and the planet, from possible irreversible damage.

Challenges

Implementing any of the sustainable development goals is easier said than done. It is not a straightforward effort, especially when it comes with the reality of who can be tasked with the responsibility of ensuring everyone is on the same page. Pluralistic societies mean that not all will agree to one common goal and purpose. National interests and priorities, red tape, and bureaucracy will persist, along with an allocation of resources. When it comes to public funds, there will be conditions and preferences. The cascading effect may not go as planned, with smaller allocations failing to reach economically targeted groups.

It is realistic to expect that no country can meet the highest moral and ethical standards demanded of it, including a specific allocation of resources. Each country has its own conditions and priorities, by the very nature of its own sovereignty and independence. What is acceptable to one may not be acceptable to another.

Even the efforts towards a universal set of human rights, social responsibilities and standards requires that each member state allow time for adjustment and acceptance. Then there is the challenge of traditional bias and values. There is also a deep-rooted societal bias and prejudice in customs, practices, and gender treatment within each social system.

The third hurdle is that of the politicised nature of public policy. There are prevailing problems of corruption and bribery which are widespread in some governments, particularly in less-developed countries. Public abuse, lack of transparency, and use of power by government officials on state-owned resources for personal gain can be so widespread as to be an obstacle for real change.

The World Bank identifies corruption as a major challenge to its goal of eradicating extreme poverty by 2030. The bank sees removal of poverty as one of the strategic planks of its sustainable development goals (SDGs). The problem of corruption is not only impeding the benefits from reaching target groups but also worsening social problems.

Convergence

The SDGs will give rise to a possible convergence of public policy and compliances among governments towards common standards and benefits. Competing objectives can be gradually removed if SDGs are repositioned strategically and practically to serve the needs of grassroots communities and residents.

Not many will complain if public policy is enforced to reduce sources of air pollution from factories, transport, and unethical burning of forests. A study in 2017 from *Lancet* estimates that pollution is responsible for 9 million premature deaths a year, costing USD 5 trillion. In their book *The Future Is Faster Than You Think*, Peter Diamandis and Steven Kotler mention greenhouse gas as one of the biggest dangers but also point to chemicals in rivers, plastic waste in oceans and on land, and harmful particulates in the air. They acknowledge the environment problem is one of enforcement and priorities versus the vested interests of a few.

For SDGs to be successful, convergence of common goals and directions must take place. But there has to be flexibility allowing different strengths to be deployed. Any intervention at this level will require a strategic alliance among important stakeholders, bringing on board a multi-stakeholder approach allowing necessary expertise and resources towards the implementation of adaptation policies and actions. To overcome the various constraints, global-community leaders must accept the political sensitivity and pressure from interest parties. Priority including a give and take attitude must be given to a healthy, sustainable earth.

Leadership

Governments stand to have a more realistic chance of success. There is obviously legitimacy and rationale in its role to take on more proactive leadership to drive responsibly and accountably for change. As demonstrated in so many cases, governments play a key role in achieving development goals and targets through, for instance, setting, implementing, and enforcing public and social policies; establishing proper and accountable policy frameworks and standards; and regulating public utilities, from social policies to waste management and even improvements to safeguard the quality of air and water.

Governments must learn not only to make climate-related considerations a top and legal priority in their planning and development policy—very much the same emphasis they have placed on the actions against the spread of Covid-19 but also incorporate a host of interdependencies among the sustainability drivers. The experience of the Maldives, an island state with slightly more than half a million inhabitants, reminds us of the importance of government in sustainable development. The Maldives remains vulnerable to a rising sea level and a host of sustainability challenges. In addition to ensuring economic survival of its fishing and tourism sectors, the government already has its hands full managing the challenges of fresh water, energy, and waste management. There are already efforts made, and its challenges are no different from others.

There are several lessons to learn from the variety of initiatives, treaties, coalitions, and reports that have been written over the past three decades, from the early years when international policy on mitigation of climate change was tabled at the Kyoto Protocol in 1997 and a nonbinding agreement made under the United Nations Framework Convention on Climate Change to reduce carbon emissions of those countries that ratified it. The agreement among advanced nations was concluded in 2005, but since then, it has been superseded by the 2016 Paris Agreement that commits all nations to keep the rise in global warming to well below 2 °C above preindustrial levels and to pursue efforts to limit the increase to 1.5 °C, recognizing that this would substantially reduce the risks and impacts of climate change.

By the very nature and influence of government, and its access to power, intelligence and resources, it is right to say that governments would have an important responsibility to flatten the climate curve, a view that was strongly expressed in the *Economist* issue of 23 May 2020. Governments do have the mandate and the power to plan and realise developmental objectives and targets, especially SDGs. Effective implementation of such ambitious goals would demand governments to effectively lead and steer.

A new framework may eventually emerge to bind nations to a more realistic target—perhaps not 2 °C as planned but preparing for a scenario for a warmer earth of 3 or 4 °C higher. Such a scenario can only mean more adaptation practices to cope with extreme weather, prolonged droughts, severe flooding, or forest fires. It also may involve more frequent outbreaks of new pandemics or health crises. No political leaders will want to turn away populist policies that play an essential role in shaping and improving people's lives.

One such example is seen in the economic stimulus packages announced by governments all over the world to jumpstart their sluggish economies following the impact of the global Covid-19 pandemic. The stimulus packages worth billions were aimed at reactivating domestic economies to save jobs. A consistent view among many experts was that governments should deliberately chart a new direction that places greater promotion of green recovery in stimulus packages through climate-friendly technologies and helping the private sector align business recovery with green initiatives and investments.

More and more CEOs are telling their governments that economy recovery packages must include low-carbon investment that leads to better efficiency and opportunities for new employment and better returns. One such example was reported in the *Guardian* on 5 May 2020; the British government was reminded of the good examples of projects on energy efficiency, infrastructure for homes, protecting homes from floods, and so on. This was based on an Oxford University study suggesting that any adaptation solutions must commit to cutting carbon emissions in line with the Paris Agreement. The economic benefits of decarbonisation exercises, renewable energy, electric vehicles, and other clean technology must be part of the green recovery.

Nonetheless, much more is expected from the business sector. According to the draft UN report *Uniting Business in the Decade of Action*, the pace of change and actions to meet the SDGs by 2030 are below expectations. The report warned that 46 per cent of the participants who took part in the survey have embedded the principles of SDGs in their business plans. In order to realise the ambitious SDGs, a quantum leap beyond principles and policies is necessary. In other words, businesses have to put these guidelines into action.

For this to take place, governments and immediate stakeholders—including both the most advanced and wealthiest nations and emerging markets—will need to start the process of adapting and adjusting warmer climate policies, processes, and technologies to national agendas, contexts, and interests. Whether it involves helping communities with housing and community needs or adapting technologies to create value, the buy-in process is lengthy and often complex, involving political tasks to get various stakeholders' participation and create ownership. This is difficult and time-consuming.

It is the government's role to regulate and work with business partners not only on delivery but also in longer-term and nonfinancial considerations. These include the extent to which ensuring businesses operate and deliver ethically and with due consideration for the interests of the environment as well as their own employees and other stakeholders. Convergence of public policy on environmental challenges and goals can take place if policies and standards are agreed to and facilitated at every level.

Governments have access to relevant big data, and expertise on both business and social implications. They can even put forward and advocate a broad range of financial instruments, including fiscal incentives or taxes, subsidies, and incentives across economies.

Commitment

The areas in which governments should increasingly make a sustainability difference include raising greater awareness and promoting the financial consequences of social and environmental impacts and mitigation. In terms of climate change, this could be associated with allowing greater fiscal incentives or associated costs or green taxes and levies. In education, public policy should include activities of governments in addressing challenges to meet the commitment of reducing carbon footprint. It is expected that governments in advanced nations will continue to review and introduce green taxes to discourage fossil fuel–driven economies.

A whole host of stakeholders have played a prominent role in these efforts over the last decades, helping to raise awareness among businesses of the importance of sustainability issues. National governments have the compliance power to take legal action to require large businesses and government bodies to play their part in protecting the environment.

Driving the importance of transparency remains one of the convergence actions. Sustainability reporting has been made simpler and easier, with better awareness of issues involving responsible use of natural resources, potential polluting activities, and environmental impact. Governments can or should increasingly make a difference in the global battle with key issues such as climate change, water and air pollution, and the plastic menace.

Consumers

One of the convergence trends involves educating consumers that a throwaway lifestyle is wasteful and unnecessary. They must learn of the dangers of plastic waste, among others, and make informed choices about what products they can consume responsibly and what resources they really need.

While it may not be easy for the business community to immediately reduce the use of plastic and materials that harm the environment, consumers can make a difference on the demand side by asking for biodegradable products. The government, for its part, can make a difference by regulating the ethical part of such businesses and making it more affordable for consumers to go green. Banning the consumption of wildlife is another area of government influence, and encouraging healthier diets would be part of consumer education. Although it is hard for consumers to discard old habits, governments have a moral duty to do what is right for ecology, health, and conservation of resources.

On the Front Line

The consequences of not doing anything in the face of a growing risk of climate change, waste pollution, and pandemic are real. If these risks are not managed and addressed, there will be significant unintended consequences to the basic elements of the support system. The most basic step for sustaining the system is access to clean water, which is clearly vulnerable to the impact of climate change. Shortage of water leads to droughts and an increase in heat-related deaths and illness, as well as vector-borne diseases such as malaria and dengue fever.

Rising sea levels caused by the melting polar ice caps poses a danger to low-lying countries and calls for enforced coastal protection, especially for small islands and large coastal cities. Estimates have been made that, within fifty years, around 200 million people could be displaced by rising water levels. Developing countries and communities are, by nature, more dependent on agriculture, which is vulnerable to increasing temperatures or flooding, leading to increased poverty and an inability to be self-sustaining.

Against this background, governments should be positioned to push sustainability issues to the forefront. The leadership role at a policy level is necessary and consistent with regulatory support and enforcement. Working on scientific statistics is a necessary success factor towards conserving and using natural resources sustainably.

It is an uneasy and probably impossible task for all governments to converge on a common line of action. But governments must recognise that they are the front-liners in championing the sustainability agenda. Not only can they make a difference to the preservation of ecology and environmental-impact differences, the deployment and enforcement of policy does make a difference. There will be a need to persuade reluctant nations that may not share common ideals and aspirations, which clearly means that those who are in front of the agenda would need to do more.

At no time in the history of humanity has there been a more urgent need for an increased convergence and cooperation at global levels for concerted action among community leaders towards governing and creating a change in business and social behaviours that can and will make a difference to a sustainable future.

There is enough evidence that governments partnering within a broad range of stakeholders can meet this expectation. Failure to do so will leave the fragile earth in a more fractured state and make it harder to repair. The clock is already ticking.

ABOUT THE AUTHORS

Tay Kay Luan is the vice chancellor of the International University of Malaya-Wales. He is a member of the board of trustees for Yayasan Astro Kasih. He authored recent publications entitled *Applying Sustainability Principles and Practices* and *Perspectives on Social and Business Sustainability*. He graduated from the London School of Economics and Political Science and Kingston University London.

Zubair Hassan teaches at the International University of Malaya-Wales. He specialises in management studies, leadership, marketing, and human resources. He is a graduate of Monash University in Australia with a master's in public policy and management.

www.ingramcontent.com/pod-product-compliance
Lightning Source LLC
Chambersburg PA
CBHW030932180526
45163CB00002B/545